RAISING CALM KIDS
IN A WORLD OF WORRY

Ashley Graber, LMFT, and Maria Evans, LMFT, are seasoned child and family psychotherapists and parent coaches dedicated to reducing worry in this generation and beyond. Drawing from their clinical expertise, they developed the SAFER Parenting philosophy, empowering families to implement changes that cultivate lasting calm. Through global parenting groups and speaking events, they provide practical strategies for parents to help their children navigate a world of complex, ever-changing demands. Graber and Evans have trained thousands of child therapists and taught psychology and mindfulness from grade school to graduate-level classes. They are passionate about ensuring that every family has access to the insights they need for emotional well-being.

Ashley Graber, MA, LMFT (#93479), and Maria Evans, MA, LMFT (#126113), are Licensed Marriage and Family Therapists.

Raising Calm Kids
in a World of Worry

*Tools to Ease Anxiety
and Overwhelm*

• • •

Ashley Graber, LMFT, and
Maria Evans, LMFT

THE OPEN FIELD / PENGUIN LIFE

PENGUIN BOOKS
An imprint of Penguin Random House LLC
penguinrandomhouse.com

The Open Field/A Penguin Life Book

THE OPEN FIELD is a registered trademark of MOS Enterprises, Inc.

Title page illustration by Alexis Seabrook

Set in FS Brabo Pro
Designed by Sabrina Bowers

LIBRARY OF CONGRESS CATALOGING-IN-PUBLICATION DATA
Names: Graber, Ashley, author. | Evans, Maria (Psychotherapist), author.
Title: Raising calm kids in a world of worry : tools to ease anxiety
and overwhelm / Ashley Graber and Maria Evans.
Description: [New York] : The Open Field/Penguin Life, [2025] |
Includes index. | Summary: "Psychotherapist and parent coach team
Ashley Graber and Maria Evans show parents how to help their
anxious children tame worry, build newfound confidence, and develop
into joyful, resilient humans" —Provided by publisher.
Identifiers: LCCN 2024022660 (print) | LCCN 2024022661 (ebook) |
ISBN 9780143137795 (paperback) | ISBN 9780593511909 (ebook)
Subjects: LCSH: Anxiety in children. | Calmness. |
Resilience (Personality trait) in children. | Parenting.
Classification: LCC RJ506.A58 G73 2025 (print) | LCC RJ506.A58 (ebook) |
DDC 618.92/8522—dc23/eng/20241105
LC record available at https://lccn.loc.gov/2024022660
LC ebook record available at https://lccn.loc.gov/2024022661

Printed in the United States of America
1st Printing

MARIA SHRIVER

PRESENTS

THE OPEN FIELD

A PUBLISHING IMPRINT

BOOKS THAT RISE ABOVE THE NOISE AND MOVE HUMANITY FORWARD

Dear Reader,

Years ago, these words attributed to Rumi found a place in my heart:

> *Out beyond ideas of*
> *wrongdoing and rightdoing,*
> *there is a field. I'll meet you there.*

Ever since, I've cultivated an image of what I call "the Open Field"—a place out beyond fear and shame, beyond judgment, loneliness, and expectation. A place that hosts the reunion of all creation. It's the hope of my soul to find my way there—and whenever I hear an insight or a practice that helps me on the path, I love nothing more than to share it with others.

That's why I've created The Open Field. My hope is to publish books that honor the most unifying truth in human life: We are all seeking the same things. We're all seeking dignity. We're all seeking joy. We're all seeking love and acceptance, seeking to be seen, to be safe. And there is no competition for these things we seek—because they are not material goods; they are spiritual gifts!

We can all give each other these gifts if we share what we know—what has lifted us up and moved us forward. That is our duty to one another—to help each other toward acceptance, toward peace, toward happiness—and my promise to you is that the books published under this imprint will be maps to the Open Field, written by guides who know the path and want to share it.

Each title will offer insights, inspiration, and guidance for moving beyond the fears, the judgments, and the masks we all wear. And when we take off the masks, guess what? We will see that we are the opposite of what we thought— we are each other.

We are all on our way to the Open Field. We are all helping one another along the path. I'll meet you there.

Love, *Maria S.*

To our parents:

Luba, Scott, Stan and Kay

Contents

Introduction

Becoming a parent is like carrying a backpack full of the most significant responsibilities you've ever had. When your child is born, you immediately feel the urge to protect them from all of life's unexpected ups and downs. You keep adjusting the straps, hoping to get comfortable with the weight as you move forward. You strive to keep them safe at every turn, but the journey can feel heavy. We're here to help lighten the load, guiding you every step of the way.

Watching your child grow brings about so much joy and equal parts worry over their unpreventable hurts. Witnessing their anxieties can be painful, confusing, and sometimes frustrating. Every parent has wondered at one time or another if they cause their child's struggles. Caregivers often believe they should instinctively know all about child-rearing and feel guilty when they don't get it right.

The reality is, parenting is a skill learned on the job, and that rarely comes easily, especially if no one has shown you the ropes. Moms and dads (and a few grandparents and other caregivers) join our parenting groups out of a desperate need for change. They discover effective tools to help their children, and they find relief in knowing that all parents struggle with what to do and say, regardless of how composed things may appear on the outside.

But raising children is getting harder as anxiety levels keep climbing, even among the youngest kids. The mental health crisis facing children has escalated sharply in recent years, with millions from the ages of 3 to 17 receiving diagnoses for ADHD, anxiety, behavioral problems, or depression, often with multiple conditions occurring together.[*] Suicidal behaviors among teens have also surged, bringing profound heartache to families.[†]

These trends mirror what we see as parenting coaches. Over the years, we've worked with thousands of parents and children struggling with anxiety and stress. What we know for sure is: families need better ways to find calm. To meet that need, we developed the SAFER Parenting philosophy to help parents navigate children's biggest anxieties in a world that seems to have an endless supply of them.

In the chapters ahead, we use the words "stress," "worry," and "anxiety" interchangeably to show that these are everyday feelings, not just clinical terms. When we mention anxiety or say someone is feeling anxious, we're talking about the feelings of unease or stress that everyone experiences, not necessarily a diagnosed condition. Every child feels worry, stress, or anxiety at some point, and this book is here to help you manage those moments. Whether your child deals with these feelings once in a while or more often, the tips and strategies we share will be useful for you both.

---

[*] "Data and Statistics on Children's Mental Health," Centers for Disease Control and Prevention, last reviewed March 8, 2023, https://www.cdc.gov/childrens mentalhealth/data.html.
[†] Agency for Healthcare Research and Quality (US), *2022 National Healthcare Quality and Disparities Report* (Rockville, MD: Agency for Healthcare Research and Quality, 2022), https://www.ncbi.nlm.nih.gov/books/NBK587182.

We've written this book with parents of 6-to-12-year-olds in mind; however, our insights and strategies provide valuable guidance on nurturing and supporting your child at any age.

What Is SAFER Parenting?

Kids do well and build emotional strength when they have supportive caregivers and feel safe. In other words, the answer to easing your child's worries in many ways is right here—it's you! You can be that dependable person during their early years as they start exploring the world and encounter things that upset them or make their eyes go wide. And when you think, "I can't control everything happening out there," you can say to yourself, "But they have me! I'm here to support them, love them, and help them learn to handle their feelings."

You may be wondering, why "SAFER"? At its core, our approach involves coaching parents to provide their children with psychological safety. The safer a parent you can be for your child, the better. This sense of security is not just derived from one thing—sometimes, this means a Band-Aid and a kiss on the knee; other times, it involves shielding them from an angry adult. It's about letting your child be furious and cry over something trivial, knowing it won't matter the next day. It's about showing up for a tough conversation, calm and ready to listen.

We've broken down the elements of SAFER Parenting into five principles: Set the Tone, Allow Feelings to Guide Behaviors, Form Identity, Engage Like a Pro, and Role Model. Collectively, these principles make up a roadmap to help parents create a safe environment for children and ease their worries.

S | *Set the Tone*

This is the first and most foundational principle. Setting a calm tone involves regulating your own emotions, because your ability to find calm helps your child find theirs. When you Set the Tone, you:

+ Discover how to manage your own reactivity constructively

+ Create an emotionally safe environment for your child

+ Help children feel more at ease when discussing challenging topics

+ Become the most composed person in any situation, where your calm aids your child in finding their own

A | *Allow Feelings to Guide Behaviors*

Every parent wants to know what to do and say when their child has big feelings. We'll show you how to steer them toward alternative behaviors instead of scolding and punishing; and when things don't go well, how to repair the situation. When you Allow Feelings to Guide Behaviors, you:

+ Teach your child to identify and articulate their feelings

+ Foster a mind-body connection and teach calming tools

+ Prepare your child for future challenges with a Plan to Cope (PTC)

- Learn the golden rule for handling emotions (spoiler: guide the behavior, not the feeling)

F Form Identity

Cultivating a strong sense of self is essential for a child's emotional well-being. We'll guide you in acknowledging their strengths, improving your relationship, and anchoring them in your family heritage and broader community. When you help to Form Identity, you:

- Help your child build sturdy self-confidence for their lifetime

- Provide your child with resilience against peer pressure

- Strengthen your bond for a solid parent-child connection

- Cultivate your child's sense of belonging

E Engage Like a Pro

This principle teaches you the tools we, as psychotherapists, use to effectively navigate conversations with children. You'll learn communication strategies that make you the trusted person your child can approach to discuss any topic. When you Engage Like a Pro, you:

- Use techniques to encourage children to share more

- Help your child's worries dissipate by having productive conversations

- Identify the best moments to initiate and sustain conversations

- Avoid typical responses that shut kids down or make things worse

R Role Model

To create a calm environment for your child, you need to closely examine your own behaviors that might inadvertently increase their anxiety. This principle will help you assess how you manage stress and its impact on your children, encouraging you to adopt healthier ways to cope. When you Role Model, you:

- Demonstrate good coping habits in front of your child

- Model positive self-esteem to nurture your child's inner voice

- Address emotional challenges of loved ones in age-appropriate ways

- Create a plan for yourself to address deeper challenges

The SAFER Parenting philosophy can be embedded in how you parent daily, how you talk to your kids, and how you carry yourself. Think of it as a layer of protection against life's biggest anxieties. Each of the five principles promotes emotional safety, and the more you incorporate these into your parenting, the more effective you will be at helping your children manage worry.

Child therapy works because it offers kids a safe, secure place to sort through their worries. Similarly, our philosophy aims to create the same kind of calm, predictable space. It ensures that your child recognizes you as an approachable and reliable figure they can depend on, no matter what they are going through. That's the primary goal of SAFER Parenting.

Psychological Safety

One night in our weekly parenting group, Angela, admittedly anxious, said, "This kind of protection is totally foreign to me. We all loved each other a lot, but my parents never tried to make me feel emotionally safe. Dad worked, and Mom seemed overwhelmed with the three of us kids. They never asked me what was wrong when I needed them or tried to help me feel better. I don't think they knew how." This family had love but lacked psychological safety. We want your children to know something different.

When you make your relationship psychologically safe, children can navigate their changing moods and behaviors more easily. They learn to communicate their feelings instead of letting them explode or bottling them up. These skills help them grow into adults who know who they are, what's important to them, and how to advocate for their needs.

With your support, they feel accepted and valued for their unique identity. They develop higher confidence in their abilities and stronger self-esteem. The bond you build with your child will result in more conversations where they seek your guidance. They also perform better academically, as feeling secure allows them to focus on learning without being distracted by emotional stressors. With a foundation of love and acceptance, you're raising kids who aren't just smart but happy, self-knowing, and resilient.

Children who experience this kind of safety grow up to be adults who opt for a walk when feeling overwhelmed instead of downing a second beer to numb discomfort. They maintain solid relationships with friends and intimate partners, having learned healthy conflict resolution from you. Comfortable in seeking support from others during stress, they are likely to experience fewer mental health issues and are better protected against severe anxiety.

Today, you can find a ton of information on social media or online about what to say to children when they are worried, but to build true emotional and psychological safety, you need more than just clever phrases. You need to create the conditions for emotional comfort and ease. By embodying the principles of SAFER Parenting, you become a beacon of the stability and reassurance you wish existed in the world.

It's true that a bit of worry is normal and even useful. It helps kids spot dangers and keep themselves from harm. Without some concern, they might not think about the risks of playing outside during a thunderstorm or approaching a dangerous animal. A little anxiety also teaches kids about their limits and encourages them to say no to risky situations, like trying a weed pen. But sometimes, it can feel like too much and they become overwhelmed by worry. The tools we offer here will help them manage big emotions so they can get back to being kids.

Not Just Another Parenting Style

Parenting has come a long way from the days when children were raised to be "seen and not heard." Top-down family setups, where parents knew best, have given way to a greater emphasis on understanding and meeting children's needs. That's a good thing. This change is driven by psychologically informed methods that value and prioritize a close parent-child relationship. Even so, some of the people we work with grew up in homes where a "hands-off" type of parenting was the norm, with little to no structure or rules. Or, conversely, some parents were so enmeshed in their kids' lives, there was barely room to think. No wonder so many people are utterly confused about which parenting style is right, especially as parenting gets more and more complex (thanks a lot, smartphones and scary headlines!).

No doubt, how you were raised influences how you parent. Maybe you follow the rules and values you grew up with, or you might run away from those models as a reaction. And whichever parenting style you choose, it's bound to cause conflict at some point between partners and co-parents who were raised differently.

If you have more than one kid, it only gets trickier since you never get the same parenting experience twice. Gabrielle, like so many parents, tells us that her daughter will "get over" disappointment quickly while her son can't stop crying, or that one child listens when they ask them to clean up while the other just outright ignores them. Each child experiences a different side of you as a parent, too, since you're at a different place in your life and every relationship has unique joys and challenges.

Despite the many changes in parenting philosophies over the years, we now recognize the fundamental role you play in influencing your child's anxiety levels. By applying the SAFER Parenting principles, you equip your children with the skills to navigate life's twists and turns. While you cannot shield your children from every hardship, you can certainly prepare them to manage stress more effectively by creating a safe environment at home.

Establishing a stable environment for your child is a culmination of decisions, both big and small. Not every home environment is safe. In such cases, alternative dependable settings, such as schools or relatives' homes, can provide the stability and calm that children need. Teachers and caregivers can also apply the tools in this book to support the children in their care.

How the Book Works

Raising Calm Kids in a World of Worry is based on our child psychotherapy and parent coaching work, which began in Los Angeles and expanded to different parts of the globe. Our weekly groups have become a treasured time for many parents who come to relate to other parents just like them and their all-too-common challenges. The hour spent together learning and growing often offsets the self-blame that always seems to pile up, no matter what they do. Parents relate to each other's struggles. Hearing others share similar experiences gives them solace that they are not alone and offers inspiration to reset and parent again the next day. Many of our groups have stayed together for years.

As you read, we want you to feel like you're right there with us in one of our parent coaching circles. We've included numerous examples throughout this book that reflect the shared experiences of families to help you feel understood and not alone in your journey. It might even feel like we've been a fly on the wall in your kitchen, as these examples capture the universal struggles and triumphs we've witnessed in our work with parents and children. Rest assured, we've changed all identifying details to protect confidentiality.

We also want to make sure you have simple, research-based strategies that are practical enough to implement immediately. Parent coaching is about quickly finding the information you need. Forget scrolling through online forums and social media groups, which can increase your anxiety. Instead, we've done the hard work of gathering all the most useful parenting practices and habits of mind. We invite you to dip in whenever you need that extra boost or want some parenting wizardry to get through a particularly rough patch. Skim it when you have, say, ten minutes before carpool pickups or before you fall asleep at night. The ideas are practical and straightforward enough to share with co-parents, grandparents, a babysitter, and everyone else involved in your children's development.

In Part I, we'll help you understand the often overlooked and misunderstood roots of your child's worry, as well as how to spot anxiety. Then, in Part II, we'll walk you through each principle of SAFER Parenting and show you how to implement it. You may not always like what we say, but trust that our tools come from coaching successes with real-life families whose lists of concerns probably look a lot like yours.

Join the Club

You're reading this book because you want to prevent your children from worrying as much as possible. We understand that. But this book isn't actually for them, it's for you. That's because when you're less anxious, your children tend to be less stressed, too—and vice versa. By learning these techniques yourself, you're managing their worry at the same time.

Parents often wrestle with guilt when they recognize the potential impact they may have on their children's anxieties. Here, we offer you the tools to confront and refine aspects of yourself that are still evolving. Acknowledging and addressing your unproductive behaviors is one of the bravest steps you can take as a parent. As you apply the tools and skills outlined in these chapters, your children will benefit from having a parent who recognizes their worries and steers them toward effective coping mechanisms.

Being a better-informed parent makes you stronger and more confident. Remember, it's never too late to turn things around. Even if you sometimes feel lost about handling your child's anxiety, this book will guide you through implementing these strategies. You can still be a great parent; armed with the right knowledge and support, you'll see just how capable you are!

SAFER Parenting is a no-judgment zone, so go easy on yourself. In coaching, there's no room for shame or blame. We pinpoint the issues, discover effective coping strategies, and build your skills until success becomes a natural part of your routine.

We laid it all out here. We're glad to have you join us.

Part I:
The What and Why of Worry

•   •   •

One

Why Kids Worry

When a child experiences worry that won't go away, parents feel overwhelmed and lost; they desperately want to make it better but don't know how. We get emails and calls from parents looking for guidance nearly every day. Paige wrote, "I'm sitting in the parking lot after drop-off, typing this email. I need your help. My daughter has good friends, but she constantly worries about people liking her. I can't convince her not to worry no matter what I say. I'm out of ideas of how to support her, and I feel her pain; I was worried as a kid, too. Please call me as soon as you can."

A child's anxiety takes a toll on everyone who loves them. Curtis said, "I'm reaching out because my son's anxiety has spiraled, and we're at a loss. It's heart-wrenching to see him suddenly consumed by fear, obsessing over animal extinction. He's also constantly anxious about the possibility of a school shooting. How should we respond? My partner and I are both on edge, we've started snapping at each other, and now we're even short with him. This feels terrible for all of us."

As psychotherapists, we consider anxiety, especially in children, a catastrophic mental health concern. For parents, the complexities have multiplied, and the challenges have expanded beyond traditional childhood worries, making the load of anxiety a collective burden that children, like everyone else, must bear. Kids encounter daily social dynamics, academic pressures, and, of course, the omnipresence of technology.

While some children may outgrow their worries, others find them persistent. In every parenting group, anxiety and overwhelm are frequent topics of discussion. "My child seems scared of everything and now avoids going to practice, even though they live for volleyball," says one mom. Another chimes in: "Yes, my son's been worried for months about being expelled, even though we've never received a single call from school!"

The first step to helping reduce the anxiety kids carry is to learn about what's contributing to it in the first place. As parents in our groups learn about the factors listed in this chapter, they begin connecting the dots for their own families. For instance, Ana told us, "It never occurred to me that my own stress about getting places on time is making my kid nervous."

Together, you and your child can develop the tools necessary to navigate the anxieties of today's world. But it starts with understanding what makes children worry. We'll teach you how to recognize these stressors and offer strategies for support. Understanding what causes kids' worries is no longer just beneficial—it's essential for effective parenting.

The Worries We See and the Worries We Don't

If your kid is afraid of spiders, you know because they squeal when they see one. You know they don't like the dark because they ask to keep a light on. But sometimes, things you can't see or may not have considered also cause worry. Your child might feel too embarrassed to tell you they're being picked on at school, or they overheard a scary piece of news they're trying to make sense of, or they're picking up on your own stress. And sometimes, children simply have no clue what is upsetting them in the moment.

Just like when we work with parents in person, the first thing we want to do is help you understand the whole picture. So, in this chapter, we will show you how to go beyond the surface of what your child is telling you and delve into the inner workings of their thoughts and feelings, where there are things that profoundly impact their sense of calm that they can't yet put into words.

We should acknowledge, of course, that genetic predispositions can impact how prone kids are to developing anxiety and how intensely they experience worry. But genetics alone does not determine a child's worry levels. Outside influences, parenting styles, family dynamics, and exposure to stressful events affect a child's anxiety. The reality is, it's rarely just one thing but a combination of elements that makes anxiety increase.

Fiona told us, "It never crossed my mind that my daughter would be worried about death when she was six years old." Veronica, another mom, said to the group, "My fear of germs is clearly why my kids won't sit down on public transportation." To help your child most, we want you to be aware of all these contributing factors. You can actually parent differently to help reduce the anxiety they carry. Understanding the causes of their worries is the first step. Let's get started.

What Your Child Hears and Sees

In this big, complicated world, kids sometimes see or hear things that even grown-ups can't fully understand. During a parenting group discussion about what makes parents anxious, one mom shared that she's at a loss for words when her son asks tough questions like why wars happen or if a natural disaster could hit them. Another parent, Fatima chimed in, "How do I explain death and aging to my fourth grader, much less AI? I feel like I need a PhD for handling these questions!"

The truth is, difficult topics are just part of life. Children often overhear adults or older siblings discussing sad or frightening world events, or they might encounter alarming statistics about climate change in science class. They pick up on conversations at home, even when you think they're not listening, and they exchange information with peers at school. Regardless of how much you attempt to shield them from distressing news, take it from two child specialists: children are in the know.

The reason why certain subjects can cause worry is because kids don't yet have the emotional sophistication to understand the nuances of a situation or a grasp on the cycle of life. They often fill in the blanks by assuming the worst. Their young minds often extrapolate from what they've heard or seen, becoming convinced that the same horrible thing will happen to them, you, or someone else they love. Therefore, it's important to be aware, as much as you can, of the kinds of information your child consumes.

Here are some of the most common ways your child might access anxiety-inducing information.

The Internet

Children's brains are not equipped to process the vast amounts of information they encounter on the internet and social media. Online, children can gain access, often accidentally, to content that's too adult for their developing brains. They can access pornography as fast as an adult by typing a word into the search bar, and without any age verification. They also can't discern an online stranger's age and intentions. The internet can be a dreadful and dangerous place for kids, especially if you don't have enough protection in place.

News

With just a glance at your cell phone, children can read a news headline or see a photo that spikes their anxiety. The news in print, on TV, and on the radio often prioritizes sensational stories covering violence, natural disasters, and horrific accidents. Children need more sophistication and context for these complicated issues that they simply don't have at this age.

Screen Time

The future was supposed to bring us jetpacks and flying cars. Instead, we got kids in the back of the minivan refusing to hand over their iPads. You don't need us to tell you that frequent screen use is habit-forming and makes children want more. But it also adds to their worries. Exposure to electronic devices for hours on end increases levels of anxiety in kids, regardless of what they're watching.

One of our clients told us, "Julian kept yelling at me when I asked him to put away his tablet. We are now only allowing an hour of screens a day outside of homework, and I swear, by day four, it's like I have a different kid. I don't recognize him. He's laughing, coming up with fun games to play, and even going outside on his own." We hear this so often from parents who continuously lament tech use as a source of strife in their homes.

Screens may provide an easy answer when there's nothing else to do, but they are not conducive to calm; they increase isolation and reduce face-to-face socialization. While focused on screens, children cannot tune into their senses and be present with their surroundings and the people around them, which is an essential aspect of reducing anxiety. The more kids use electronics, the less they engage in everything else.

No, not all time spent on electronic devices is harmful, and we don't advocate taking away screen time completely. The use of technology is valuable for education, entertainment, and communication, and kids will need it for the rest of their lives. We also know it takes a lot of work to keep kids off devices! That's why parental controls, consistent boundaries around screen time, and supervision are even more essential these days. Many parents we work with tell us that they know that keeping device use low is necessary, yet boundaries and supervision around technology are what they struggle with the most. When parents help children reduce tech use overall, and it becomes a more minor part of family life, fighting over screen time goes down, too.

AI and New Technology

Even though emerging technology like AI can be cool, the idea that it can take on human-like qualities can be overwhelming for kids. Children learn about AI as a powerful tool that can communicate, but it is so difficult for kids to understand, especially because even adults don't know where its development will go. It's easy for their minds to go to scary places, like 11-year-old Sierra, who said, "When AI improves, will it watch my every move?"

Mature Content

You undoubtedly remember seeing a movie, TV show, or magazine as a kid that was too racy, scary, or advanced for your age. Children today have infinitely more ways to access worlds beyond their comprehension. Watch out for movies, shows, books, and video games with adult content. Even though they might beg to watch something for older kids or adults, remember that ratings are there because certain themes are extra impactful on children. Being exposed to topics that are more mature than they can handle, even when they think they are old enough, causes unnecessary worry.

Mass Shootings and Other Disasters

Repeated reminders of potential violence or danger can create a sense of insecurity in children. School drills teach kids how to keep themselves safe during a shooting or earthquake, but they also serve as overwhelming reminders that a disaster could happen at any moment.

These stress responses can happen repeatedly and overload their developing nervous system, disrupting their capacity to learn. As one parent told us, "My kid is wearing a bulletproof backpack. He's finding out that people can cause harm intentionally, and that danger could arise at any moment. No wonder he's distracted in class."

Arabella, age 7, told her brother that while she sat under her desk during a drill, all she could think about was not seeing her mom again. And Enzo, age 12, told us that he is afraid that he'll breathe too loudly, and a shooter will find him. Whether they are thinking about it or not, this consistent risk of danger affects how they feel. It's anxiety-provoking for everyone.

What Your Child Experiences: The Everyday and Not-So-Everyday Stressors of Life

Sometimes in life things run smoothly, and then there are times where we are faced with changes we can't prevent. Let's examine what children might encounter and how it affects their levels of calm.

Navigating Social Dynamics

As kids grow up and begin figuring out who they are, they really start to care about what their friends think. They want to fit in and feel liked. Take the story of one kid who just wanted someone to play with. Her grandmother shared with us during a session, "Every night, she asks me, 'Nana, do you think I'll ever have a good friend?' It breaks my heart. I tell her to hang in there, but it's tough not knowing what else to say."

When children are different from their peers, whether due to their appearance, interests, cultural background, race, or any other aspect of their identity, they may worry or become the target of bullying or teasing. Hunter was harassed at his previous school for wearing nail polish, and Zienna felt terrible when a classmate pointed out that her parents have an accent. Angel, whose family moved to a small town, was not finding other Puerto Rican kids to hang out with and was worried he was not welcome like he felt in his previous school.

Aiden was diagnosed with diabetes at age 3 and had a service dog that was trained to detect unsafe changes in his blood sugar levels. As much as all the kids thought having a dog at school was incredible, it made Aiden feel separate from his friends. Being different can be a good thing, but it is not easy when you're the only one. Pay attention to whether your child is surrounded by people who are not like them in essential ways.

Social Media

Adding social media to the mix amplifies kids' worries about social dynamics and negatively impacts their self-worth. Children will compare their lives to highlight reels of friends and complete strangers, and they cannot discern what is real versus filtered or fake. In our child therapy practices, kids tell us all the time they receive hurtful messages directly from their peers, read super-offensive comments, hear about someone getting verbally harassed online, or worse.

This is also where fear of missing out comes in. Children feel excluded by seeing what others post on social media, and they begin to depend on these indicators of popularity for self-worth. With the advent of phones, kids today are pressured to "sext," which involves sending explicit images of themselves. This behavior is often the result of peer pressure to fit in or be liked by other kids. Be sure to discuss the serious consequences of sharing personal photographs with people of any age.

It's impossible to fully relax when you're checking phone notifications, relying on external validation via likes and comments. The expected proof of approval doesn't always come, and negative feedback from peers can show up instead. When kids use social media without any supervision, it really ramps up their anxiety. They might lose sleep or develop issues with self-esteem and body image, which can even spark eating disorders. They see other people's lives online and start feeling bad about their own, which makes them worry a lot more.

Body Discomfort and Developmental Changes

Childhood is all about change, especially as adolescence approaches. Pimples, weird hair on different parts of your body, smelly armpits. Experiencing physical changes can make kids more self-conscious, body-conscious, confused, and insecure. Some children are so preoccupied with weight that they must be reminded that a growing child should be getting physically bigger! Even the anticipation about these shifts can contribute to unease during this life stage. Not to mention the hormones that begin to rage. Estrogen and testosterone levels increase stress and can cause mood swings, general crankiness, and elevated worry.

Even little physical changes can be a big deal. When you wonder why your children's worry has kicked up, consider whether they might be run down from too little sleep or feeling sick. Tired kids worry more, and when kids experience body discomfort like muscle aches, fever, pain, or a rash or headache, they can become much more emotional.

Some kids worry about things that haven't even happened yet to their bodies. They might ruminate on what will happen if they get a tummy ache: will they have to take that awful-tasting pink medicine again? Or what if they get a fever that won't go down and have to skip drawing class or tae kwon do? When kids must stay home from school or miss out on events, this creates a disruption in their routine that can also magnify worry. Nia was convinced she'd fall behind when she got her second sore throat of the winter season. She repeatedly told her parents each morning, "There's no way I can catch up on homework, and my friends are going to forget I exist."

Change and Disruption

Big changes, like moving to a new house or school, can be both exciting and scary for kids. Even if the change is supposed to be a good thing, your child might feel like they're losing something before they can see the benefits. For example, before they can enjoy having a new sibling, they might feel sad about no longer being the only child. And some changes are just plain tough, with little upside—like a parent moving away, their favorite babysitter leaving, a beloved camp or team sport getting canceled, or a friend changing schools. Keep an eye out for these changes because they can really stir up worries in kids.

A Packed Schedule

Kids love to play; that's no secret. But sometimes, we adults forget to leave space for unstructured time. In families where academics, extracurriculars, and chores take priority from morning to bedtime, it leaves little room for relaxation. And when children don't take time to recharge, they are at risk of developing chronic stress.

Be sure to give your kids plenty of free playtime. It's how they learn, process emotions, and make sense of what's happening around them. For instance, after a middle-of-the-night visit to the emergency room, Aria, age 7, turned her bedroom into an ER for her "sick and injured" stuffed animals. Older kids need playtime, too—so if they're off starting a pretend Baby-Sitters Club or are in deep with art supplies drawing a card deck of knights and dragons, that's their way of learning. Leave space for them to play freely whenever you can.

Joseph, an executive who came to an online lunchtime parenting group, shared that he wasn't sure how to unwind because he grew up in a deeply serious family where play was never encouraged, and they hardly ever laughed together. He said that now, as an adult, having an afternoon with no plans made him uncomfortable. It wasn't the first time we heard this. Children need downtime, and so do you. Downtime isn't a luxury; it's a necessity for everyone in your family, for both physical and mental health.

Inconsistency

Kids feel secure when they know what's coming next. While you can't always control when life gets thrown off, an ongoing lack of consistency in your child's routine will lead to stress. For example, Crystal, age 9, told us, "I wish things weren't so different each day. Mom always changes plans in the morning, and I feel like my whole day is broken." Things don't need to be the same all the time, but last-minute changes in their daily schedule will make kids nervous. Having a caregiver who is often late or says they will be there and then doesn't show up may cause anxiety in a child, too.

In the same way, when a child receives conflicting signals from each of their grown-ups, or when rules and expectations change from day to day, children experience a sense of discomfort. Children enjoy it when they get permission to stay up late on a special occasion, but too many ten p.m. bedtimes invariably escalate anxiety.

Trauma

Every family goes through tough times; you might be facing one right now. Some things that affect your child are out of your hands, and that's a hard fact for any parent to swallow. But understanding trauma can really help you in parenting.

Trauma is the emotional and psychological impact left by a one-time incident or series of painful or harmful experiences. It can leave a child feeling devastated, scared, or hurt, and it's tough for them to calm down because it triggers their body's stress response, sometimes known as the "fight-flight-freeze" effect.

This makes them super alert and unable to relax, constantly worried about their safety.

Even small incidents can shake a child's sense of safety. A dog bite, a car accident, or seeing someone get hurt can deeply affect them. Later, they might see something that reminds them of the event and feel scared all over again. For instance, Logan saw his grandma leave in an ambulance at age 4. Now, at 6 years old, he still gets scared when he hears an ambulance and asks each family member if they're OK.

Big stressors like natural disasters or financial troubles can also trigger trauma, especially if kids are aware of the family's struggles. Trauma can also come from ongoing issues like neglect or abandonment by a parent, domestic violence, or bullying.

Systemic racism, discrimination, and prejudice create a challenging reality for children as they navigate their early years. They face oppression through ongoing experiences that make them feel targeted for their appearance, skin color, hair texture, accent, and more. Kids tell us they fear being disliked, excluded from peer groups, or even violently attacked by others who see them as a threat or just different. This ongoing anxiety can lead to feelings of alienation and may cause children to internalize the racist attitudes directed at them, believing there is something inherently wrong with themselves and that the rejection they face is something they deserve. Continual exposure to such stress can significantly impact long-term physical and emotional well-being.

Any kind of physical discipline can also contribute to long-term trauma and high levels of anxiety. Studies consistently highlight the harmful effects of physical punishment, reinforcing our commitment to an alternative, compassionate approach that helps parents learn new communication patterns and skillful ways to guide their children's behaviors, which is exactly what you are learning here.

If a child's body is violated or touched in inappropriate ways, it completely strips away their sense of security, leaving them in a constant state of fear and worry. Untreated, this kind of trauma can cause serious long-term issues, like anxiety, depression, or thoughts of suicide. For parents, acknowledging the reality of abuse is incredibly challenging, especially if they feel guilty or have experienced abuse themselves. The first hurdle is admitting the painful truth of what is happening. As difficult as it is, mustering the courage to take action is the most critical step in safeguarding your child's future. If you suspect or know that your child is being abused in any way, we urge you to seek immediate consultation with a psychotherapist who specializes in trauma.

Divorce

Divorce can really shake things up for kids and leave them struggling in turmoil. Even when it's done amicably, some kids can't help but stress over what's going to happen next. A mom in our group, Eleni, talked about this one evening. Even though she and her ex-wife separated without much duress, the kids are still worrying about everything, from who will read to them at night to whether they can have friends over at their mom's new apartment on the weekends.

Kids can worry about divorce even when it's not likely. After hearing her dad yell at her mom one night for getting an expensive parking ticket, Audrey, age 8, assumed her parents would be breaking up. "What can I do to be sure Mommy isn't going to leave?" she asked her dad.

Sometimes, kids can take on unnecessary guilt or responsibility. Zara, age 7, told her dad she wished she hadn't argued with her sister so much, because then he wouldn't have moved out. Children are more egocentric at younger ages, meaning they can think they are the cause and reason for certain things happening. Over time, their brain develops the ability to understand cause and effect, as well as the complexity of social dynamics.

When Health Challenges Hit Home

If someone in your family is sick, it can be really hard to handle and make everyone anxious. Eleven-year-old Mateo had belly-aches for months before the doctors figured out he was allergic to gluten. That whole time of not knowing what was wrong was tough on his family. Even after he knew, Mateo was still nervous about eating the right things. His mom continued to feel anxious about what he ate most days, which also impacted his sense of calm.

Understandably, children who grow up with parents or close family members facing health concerns, physical ailments, or mental health challenges would experience worry. Certainly, a child with a parent suffering from a chronic illness and undergoing frequent hospitalizations is likely to feel anxious, worrying that their parent may become sicker or even pass away. Mental illness is no different. Children often worry about their parents' well-being and may also fear that they might be the cause of their parents' distress.

The reality is, in our parenting groups, almost every person or their spouse has *something* they are dealing with, be it an eating disorder, radiation treatment, chronic back pain, high blood pressure, or a bipolar diagnosis. Others have addictions, migraines, or something else. Many people have a few health challenges at once. It's nothing to be ashamed of; this is a part of life. But bear in mind that your child might need some extra support in coping with these situations. Managing personal adversity while raising a child is one of the most challenging things you can do as a parent. You deserve to get the support you need as much as your children do.

Learning About Death

Haruto, age 10, couldn't sleep after finding out that his best friend's brother had contracted meningitis as a toddler, thinking he or his dad could also get sick or die. When Valeria, age 8, heard about basketball player Kobe Bryant tragically dying in a helicopter alongside his daughter, she became terrified of flying.

Experiencing death, whether it's that of a great-grandparent or a beloved pet, is a powerful and potentially overwhelming experience for children. When a significant presence in a child's life is gone, regardless of the reason, most children experience a deep sense of loss and might fear the same could happen to them or you. Dying is as complicated a topic for children as it is for adults. This is the time in life when children learn that mortality is a universal aspect of the human experience, and tragically, sometimes, is the result of deliberate harm. It's frightening to think that people can do awful and evil things to others; we can all understand that.

Your Connection to Your Child

As you're discovering, life's various disruptions can amplify anxiety and worry in your child. Some of these—your child's routine and schedule—you have some control over. But for most—unexpected illness, divorce, a car accident—you do not. But here's the good news: a nurturing, empathic relationship with you is a significant source of calm in the face of what life throws at them inside and outside the home. The strong bond you develop offers them a deep sense of belonging and allows them to explore the world with a strong foundation of emotional security.

Children need to feel the devotion and affinity of a parent, a never-ending love and admiration. Their brains are wired to seek your acceptance. They pay attention to you. They watch and wonder what you think. You matter a lot to them. Even if they may not hop onto your lap to snuggle or might push you away when you try to kiss them goodbye, kids feel more prepared to endure what is anxiety-provoking or overwhelming if they know they always have you firmly in their corner.

In the coming chapters, you will learn to show your child that you have their back through and through. But first, let's examine what can get in the way of that and kick up worry.

Not Accepting Differences

In a wintertime parenting group session, a mom named Tanya told us that as a child, she was in every school play, often as the lead, and treasured this experience so much. Still, despite many attempts to change her daughter's mind about performing, she insisted on being in tech. Tanya shared with the group, "I just loved singing, dancing, and the comradery, but my daughter prefers boring lighting and set design. I don't get why she doesn't want to have the same experience—it was so fun!"

Your children may have interests, abilities, or qualities that differ from yours. Perhaps you want your child to love sports, but they are into video games, or you want them to have an adventurous spirit, but they would rather stay under the covers reading Magic Tree House books. Some kids worry that if they disappoint their parents, they won't love them the same way.

Your child's body type might differ from what you had as a kid or from what you have now. Kids are acutely aware if someone in the family seems to have things come more effortlessly to them academically, physically, or socially. Children tell us every week that they feel immense pressure to perform well in school, sharing ongoing concerns about meeting the desires of their parents and teachers.

Pushing them too far from what they like or what feels safe can backfire. When a child is compelled to do something that feels overly difficult too often, it can make them less courageous and more worried about trying new things.

If you're finding it challenging to understand or embrace your child's sexual orientation or gender identity, that can have a deep impact. Your kid values your approval more than anything, and without it, they might hide who they really are to avoid losing your love. This act of hiding can crush them inside, causing deep shame and self-loathing that can lead to dangerous behaviors, including thoughts of hurting themselves or suicide. It's essential for their well-being that they feel accepted and supported by you, just as they are.

Being Overly Critical

In parenting group one night, Jill described her children's grand-mother as a "control freak." She demonstrated to the group how frantic her mom would get, waving her hands around as she said, "With my mom, I never felt like I could do anything right. 'Sit up straight, you look like a slob hunched over; don't eat so fast, it's not a race; get your shoes on, but not those shoes, they are disgustingly dirty.' I can still hear her voice in my head as she barked orders."

We can recognize how stressed Jill's mother must have been, but it came out in judgmental tones, which hurt her as a child. In the same way, if a child is put under a microscope and expected to do things perfectly, worry rises because they so often won't live up to the task. Jill said her mother's scrutiny would make her question herself and fear she'd say the wrong thing, even in other settings. These feelings of shame are a typical result of growing up hearing antagonistic or disapproving statements from parents.

Children with highly critical parents learn to be cautious of the adults around them and live in fear of their disapproval. They may become more private about their emotional life, which also leads to festering worry and loneliness. Of course, we know that backing off from criticism isn't always easy, especially if you grew up being criticized by a parent, too. But remember, fault-finding gets in the way of your connection and increases anxiety.

Transferring Worry

Worry tends to be contagious; one person's anxiety can easily amplify another's. Children often look to adults for cues on safety, so a worried parent can inadvertently foster anxiety in their child. As a parent reflected on growing up in what she described as a "neurotic household," she said, "My mom worried about our health; she was afraid people would break into our house, or that my dad wouldn't get home for whatever reason. Now that I am really thinking about it, it was like constantly impending doom in our house."

Moreover, when a parent consistently exhibits anxiety, it not only signals to the child that their environment is unsafe, but it may also burden them with the feeling that they need to take care of the worried parent. If a child grows up thinking their role is to support a parent emotionally, they might neglect their own needs, resulting in anxiety.

Having been part of our group for a while, Kristen understood the importance of shielding her children from her financial worries. Facing mounting bills, she shared with us her stress over the costly dance costumes her daughter needed for upcoming ballet and tap performances. "I told my daughter that I worked extra hours to pay for these outfits because I want her to value them," she said. "But I kept it to myself that I almost pulled her out of the classes completely when the academy raised its tuition prices. I didn't want her to feel the weight of that decision."

We know transferring your concern onto your child is never deliberate. Keeping track of everything that could go wrong might feel like a way of gaining control over their safety. Whether it's a current huge concern, a picked-up superstition, or a fear inherited from your own upbringing, be aware that children can absorb these feelings and carry them into their adulthood.

Sweeping Conversations Under the Rug

Kids know more than we think. Sometimes, parents find it easier to sidestep certain family issues, especially those that are complex or challenging, like your own mental health struggles, a loved one's substance abuse, or problems in your own relationships. This tendency often stems from a desire to shield them and hope that the child will worry less by not discussing the issue. But when obvious problems go undiscussed, children can feel uncertain and anxious. For example, 12-year-old Miles says, "Starting in second grade, my dad would be weirdly gone for a few nights. Mom never said a word about why or when he was coming back. He always did eventually, but I hated having him gone and worrying about when he would come back." Some parents avoid these discussions because they were not raised to confront issues openly. Yet, children need their parents to talk about difficult experiences, even when those topics are complex and unresolved. Engaging in age-appropriate dialogues can lead to children feeling more secure and less overwhelmed.

Anger and Irritation

Hanna's dad had been working with us in parent coaching on his anger. Despite remembering how hurtful it was in his own childhood, Charles found himself getting angry with his kids even when he didn't mean to. He told us, "It just flies out of my mouth.

I don't want my kids to feel bad about themselves all the time. I hated feeling that way as a kid." He told us he came from a long line of men with hot tempers. But his anger was affecting his kids.

One day, Brayden, age 9, without looking up from his Etch A Sketch masterpiece, said to his therapist, "I don't ever want to be like my dad. He's so mean, and Mom says it's a good thing I'm not moody like him." His eyes darted up nervously as he said, "Don't tell my dad I said that, OK?"

If you raise your voice at your partner or children and react in unpredictable and frightening ways, it wires your child's nervous system to be always on alert, waiting for the next bad thing to happen. Kids can fear your moods.

Criticizing the Other Parent

Be extra wary of demeaning or bad-mouthing your co-parent in front of your child. While it might feel like bonding, this places the child in the middle of adult conflicts, making them feel stuck between the two of you. You may think, "They know we love them no matter what," but children come up with all sorts of worries, like "If I'm close to Dad, will Mom be mad at me?" Children can feel protective of the other parent, even if they don't say it aloud, and may be nervous to disagree with your comments. They fear similar judgment will eventually come toward them since they share some personality traits with that parent.

• • •

Children rely on their parents to be stable and calming figures in their lives. The interactions they experience with you and other adults around them and the environment you create at home significantly impact how calm they feel and how positively they view themselves.

A self-described "skeptic," Ama told the parenting group, "I just don't want my son and me to feel bad after every interaction. It's hurting both of us, and I hate it when things get heated."

Know that SAFER Parenting is here to help you learn a different, calmer way to be that will feel better for everyone.

• • • •

Right now, you are in the information-gathering stage, and we know it might feel overwhelming. But remember, understanding the root causes of your child's anxiety is the essential first step.

If you were new to our parenting group, we would invite you to identify what's truly causing your child to worry before moving into parenting solutions. So, take a minute to consider what's going on around them. Maybe they're hearing yelling at home or having problems with classmates at school. They might have caught a glimpse of some scary headlines or are feeling picked on for the little things they do.

As we've said, a bit of worry is just part of the game. Kids deal with dizzying changes all the time—new teachers, tests, shifting friendships, and simply growing up. Our SAFER Parenting approach can help your kids stay chill even when life spins them sideways. Using what you learn from this book, especially when times get tough, will help your kids feel less anxious. Your care and understanding are their best shields.

Now that you've got a clue about what might be stirring up

worry for your child, the next thing we'll get into is how to recognize the signs of anxiety as they pop up.

But before we move on, we'd like you to reflect for a moment on the most important themes from the pages you just read. You'll see questions like the ones below at the end of each chapter. We encourage you to find a quiet moment—"Yeah, right," we hear you saying—and imagine we're there with you as your supportive and encouraging parenting coaches. Try to view yourself as we would—with compassion, kindness, and open-mindedness. This is all part of your process of becoming a wiser, better-equipped, and, above all, calmer parent. We know you've got this!

Questions and Reflections
for Deeper Thinking

• Reflect on your family dynamics. Are there ongoing stresses within the family that could be contributing to your child's worries?

• Have there been any significant changes, losses, or traumas in your child's life that have impacted them recently or in the past?

• What types of news, video games, or media are impacting your child?

• Consider your own role: What might you be doing as a parent that contributes to your child's anxiety? What are you expecting them to adapt to that might be overwhelming for them?

• Looking ahead, are there upcoming changes to prepare for and tell your child about?

Two

How to Spot Worry

Anxiety presents itself in many different ways. Children don't ask, "Are we there yet?" for the seventh time to bug you, but to temper worried feelings underneath. They don't refuse to get out of the car at softball practice after saying they wanted to go in order to be difficult, but because they're afraid something bad might happen. You may think these behaviors are unrelated or don't make much sense, but they are a sign that something doesn't feel safe to your child.

In her second year as a SAFER Parent, one of our group participants said, "My husband and I had no idea some of our daughter's behaviors were signs of her worrying. We genuinely thought she was trying to manipulate a situation to avoid doing things she didn't like. Realizing that it was actually anxiety gave me so much more compassion. It's helping me stay calm more often when she's super anxious about her performances or assignments."

Having worked with thousands of families over the years, we've identified the most common symptoms and behaviors of anxiety. Some may be more obvious to you, and others may surprise you. Knowing how to spot worry is necessary to apply the

SAFER Parenting principles. No matter where you are, know that by learning this information, you're on your way to becoming attuned to what your child needs, which means you are already helping your family to have less worry.

How the Brain Amplifies Anxiety

It's helpful to know how your child's brain, particularly the amygdala and prefrontal cortex, affects their feelings. The amygdala is an ancient part of the brain that acts like an alarm system, responding to fear by preparing the body to fight, flee, or freeze—reactions that were crucial for our evolutionary ancestors, who lived among wild animals and other dangers. These automatic reactions can pose a challenge today in non-life-threatening situations, like a new school day or a stage performance. The prefrontal cortex, a more advanced area of the brain located behind the forehead, controls impulses and helps with decision-making and calming down. However, it doesn't fully mature until around age 25, which means kids struggle to think logically in stressful situations. By recognizing when your child's amygdala is running the show, you can guide them in calming down and thinking more clearly. Understanding this dynamic is a way to support your child through their anxieties, which they aren't equipped to handle alone.

＊　＊　＊

When talking with parents, we coach them to act like detectives, sniffing out clues about their kid's anxiety. Stress isn't always obvious—it can pop up in the ways your child talks, how they act, or through physical symptoms. If your child appears consistently worried or uncomfortable, or if their behavior is getting in the way of their daily life, it might be time to check in with a professional to get to the bottom of it. That's why we want you to note how often you see the signals we're about to describe. Do you notice them every day, or several times a week? Are you beginning to see patterns?

Also, keep an eye out for behaviors that need immediate attention—even if it's the first time you've noticed something, it might be a sign of a deeper issue. Kids can be really good at keeping things to themselves, and by the time they show you what's going on, it might be urgent. As you apply the SAFER Parenting principles outlined in this book, continue to assess what additional support your child might need.

It's important to keep in mind that while we're focusing on anxiety, some of these descriptions could be signs of autism or ADHD, or could indicate that your child has an underlying physical condition. In some instances, they may even be having a reaction to a medication.

We're not here to scare you—just the opposite, actually. Knowing what to look for is powerful. It's about giving you the confidence to support your child and ensure they get the help they need, when they need it. Spotting these signs early can make a huge difference in your child's well-being and is your best hope for keeping them happy and free from harm.

Worrying Out Loud

Most of the time, you'll zero in on your child's worries because they *talk about them*. They'll share their fears; and while it's perfectly normal for kids to experience anxiety as they grow, it's important to consider how often they express their worries and the extent to which they bother them. Anxieties can come up in all sorts of situations—whether your child is confronting a challenge, or when things get quiet for the day and their thoughts wander, or even seemingly out of the blue. If you notice their worries shifting rapidly from one issue to another, or if they appear especially distressed, take it as a sign that they may need additional support.

Now, let's explore how to recognize worry in the thoughts they share. .

Overthinking

Maxim, age 11, couldn't stop thinking about a disagreement with his best friend, repeating all weekend, "I don't think he'll ever hang out with me again. I don't want to lose my best friend." Even though they made up a few days later, he dwelled on it for many weeks, most nights struggling to fall asleep worrying about it.

Children like Maxim may replay thoughts and dwell on past events, regrets, or mistakes when they're anxious. They imagine what could go wrong. Future fears might sound like "I'll never be able to finish my school project in time; I have too many things to research. There's never enough time." Or "Mom, what if we get separated in a store, and I can't find you?" when that's never happened.

Sometimes, kids will chew on a topic without recognizing that it's coming from a place of anxiety, and even deny it outright. Jayden was very curious, at age 7, about mortality after his great-uncle died and talked for months about it to anyone who would listen: "Did you know that when you die, your brain stops working? Isn't that weird?" But when Jayden's mom asked him directly whether he was worried about death, he'd say, "No way." However, he could not seem to get it off his mind.

Fixation

You'll know your child is anxious about something if they become fixated on a topic or idea. Children's worry can localize on a specific subject, whether it's a genuine threat to them or not. You might wonder, "Why tsunamis and not earthquakes? We don't even have those where we live!" Some children pick up a specific worry based on their experience. For example, Stella was anxious to return to Miami—where she threw up at the hotel—for fear of getting sick again. After your child experiences a startling event or learns about something that scares them, you will know they are impacted by it if they continue to bring it up.

Sometimes, a child's worry might be about the schedule or being late. They may repeatedly ask what time it is or when something is happening, and have big feelings when plans change. Before an outing, some need to know precisely what will happen, who will be there, or whether they will be forced to try something. "What day is Grandma coming?" "Are you sure that my playdate won't get canceled?" Even after you've answered them, the questions keep coming because answering doesn't work to temper their questions or anxieties. It can be exhausting, no doubt!

When children feel scared to acknowledge something worrisome, their brains can find a different subject to agonize about. They usually don't realize they're doing it. Nine-year-old Tiffany's mind, for instance, was stuck on break-ins. Her parents were getting divorced, and her mind was gripped with "Will my home be safe?" The thought of a burglar coming through her window and grabbing her at night became the fixation instead of her parents' divorce, the actual source of her anxieties.

Many specific fears are age-appropriate and tend to go away naturally, whether it's monsters under the bed or scary TV shows. However, if your child struggles to overcome a particular fear, has trouble self-soothing, or appears more upset than usual, it might indicate a need for additional support to alleviate their worry.

Concerns About Anything and Everything

Some children worry about a handful of topics (or more) on any given day. They have fears about school today, friends on Wednesday, guitar lessons on Friday, with an extra dose of apprehension over the weekend's sleepaway plans. Their mind has a smattering of upsetting thoughts, and the anxiety jumps from one thing to another. If there's something to stress about—even if there isn't!—they are worried about it. These children imagine that something could go wrong at any point, asking, "What if there's traffic or the streetlights aren't working, or there's construction on the way again, and what if the elevator gets stuck?" The case of the "what ifs" is like having thoughts that won't stop and make them feel frightened all the time, even when there is no real danger.

Unrealistic Connections

Children sometimes believe that their thoughts, actions, or imagination have the power to influence or change events in ways that defy the laws of cause and effect. Some of this kind of "magical thinking" can be a developmentally appropriate way for kids to explain the world to themselves. Like with Cody, who imagined that he was invisible to adults when he wrapped himself in his blanket. But some can be anxiety-related if you hear your child make links between bad things transpiring or not occurring and them having something to do with it. For example, Chase believed that carrying two pebbles she found in the driveway protected her from getting hurt on the playground, and Sophia was sure she got an A+ because she wore her lucky earrings to class.

Other times, kids might have the thought that something specific needs to happen to avoid danger or that they might do something "bad." Mai, age 6, feared that she would hurt somebody without meaning or wanting to. She would hear the same thought on a loop: "You will grab them and scrape their face!" She worried it was true, even though she never scratched anyone. These thoughts can be terrifying for children. They can signal obsessive-compulsive disorder (OCD) and should be evaluated for treatment. As with all worries, consult a therapist if you see them persist.

Worst-Case-Scenario Thinking

Kids sometimes catastrophize and believe that if something can go wrong, it definitely will. For example, Colton, age 10, was worried about an upcoming trip. He'd been looking forward to going to the beach but kept saying things to Dad like "If there's a thunderstorm during our family trip, our vacation will be totally ruined and we won't have any fun. We might as well not go at all."

Worried kids may also come up with hypothetical scenarios far into the future. Twelve-year-old Kailani told her mom at breakfast, "I know I won't score during the game, and my team will lose because of me and then hate me." Then, at dinner: "I'm going to mess up my audition and then I'll never become a movie director and I'll have a terrible life."

Impractical Standards

While some level of striving for excellence is beneficial, kids who show perfectionistic tendencies offer a clue that they may be managing a great deal of worry.

Some children get frustrated easily when they make mistakes. They will focus on a stain on their shirt and easily notice flaws like if their shorts are too wrinkly or there's a freckle on their skin. They will want As at school ("Why didn't I get 100?" when they get a 98) and notice a scrap of paper on the floor and want to recycle it, even while immersed in arts and crafts. These children spend a disproportionate amount of time and effort on a task, struggle to find it "good enough," and often have difficulties completing assignments. Jordan, age 9, spends too much time on his schoolwork because he gets upset and starts the whole thing over if he makes a minor mistake.

These children often fear failure, regardless of how unlikely it is, and put incredible pressure on themselves. Ariana is an 11-year-old gymnast who berates herself if she doesn't nail the routine, even when she wins first place in a competition. Her mom said she'd spend the whole ride home saying, "I totally messed that up. Why couldn't I get my vault right? I should stop doing gymnastics. Amelia is so much better than me."

When children hold themselves to unattainable standards, they often avoid a new challenge because they fear they won't perform perfectly. They can also find it difficult to receive feedback. It's almost impossible for them to tolerate that they aren't living up to your ideals—even if you've told them otherwise—or their own. Parents with kids exhibiting these behaviors tell us their children "take things the wrong way" or "overreact to small things." You might hear, "You hate me!" when you ask them to change something minor. Mayer told us he was just trying to compliment his daughter's effort in science, and she replied, "Was I not good before?" She never thought she did anything well enough.

Negative Self-Assessment

It can be excruciating for a parent to hear their children express hostile thoughts about themselves. No matter how often Juan's mom told him how smart and loved he was, he thought differently: "They just invited me to be nice. They don't actually want me there."

Notice if your child downplays or undervalues their achievements. When Aisha gets a B+ on her math test, she says, "I always fail, and I'll never improve." When she gets an A+ in the same subject, she says, "It was just luck. Anyone could have gotten that grade."

Harmful thoughts can also be body-based thoughts, like "I'm so fat! My legs are too big, my skin is oily, and my chin sticks out!" Or you may notice your child is being tough on themselves by constantly doubting their capabilities: "There's no way I'm going to get the role in the play. I don't look the part, and I'm definitely not pretty enough." These pessimistic thoughts can be tricky to catch because while some kids speak them out loud, others keep them locked away in their minds. But no matter how these feelings get expressed, they are harsh and painful. Critical self-judgment only fuels a cycle of worry and self-doubt.

When kids have consistent negative thoughts about themselves, it could be a sign of anxiety, depression, or body dysmorphia and could warrant professional help.

Trouble Settling the Body

Bodies are great at telling us what's going on inside, especially with children. When kids are hungry, their bodies don't just sit quietly waiting for dinner; their stomachs growl, and they might start feeling cranky or dizzy. It's the same with stress. Children don't need to say out loud, "This is too much!" You can see it physically. Their cheeks might turn red, or they'll feel their heart beat faster. That's their body's way of reacting to feeling overwhelmed. It's that fight-flight-freeze response in action.

Body Cues

Sometimes, kids talk about having stomachaches or feeling queasy, or feeling like there's a lump in their throat. They might need to run to the bathroom because their tummy is either tied in knots or just the opposite. Some kids feel like they're being pressed down by a heavy weight that they just can't shake off. Bikram, age 7, told his mom he feels super sensitive to noises and lights when he's fretting about something. Watch out for these physical embodiments of worry.

Children with worry may also feel restless and have trouble sitting still. Abena, age 10, tells her dad, "I'm always antsy." Or, as Nora, age 9, said, "My leg bounces, my heart beats fast, and I feel like I can't focus in class. It's embarrassing." These kids' worries create extra energy in the body that needs help quieting down.

Anxiety Attacks

Sometimes, stress can get so ramped up inside your child's body that they will experience anxiety or a panic attack. This extreme version of worry comes up all at once, to the point where it feels terrifying for them. If you've ever had an anxiety attack, you know how awful and crippling it feels.

This level of fear can also cause children to feel sick, numb, or tingly all over their bodies. Miguel, age 12, described it this way: "I felt dizzy and couldn't breathe, then I started shaking; my thoughts were racing all over the place. I really wanted it to stop."

During a panic attack, a child may also appear frozen as the body becomes immobilized and seems stuck or unable to move. Michelle reflected on her daughter's anxiety attack in an afternoon group one day, "I could see her body was super tense; even so, her hands trembled slightly, and she even looked a little pale. She wasn't really responding to anything I was saying. It was super alarming the first couple times it happened."

These moments can be extremely frightening to you, or downright confusing. Parents sometimes tell us that the way their child describes their experience seems "over-the-top," but their symptoms really can be so severe that they can feel like they are having a heart attack. Use the tools in this book to support your child in these moments, and get a professional opinion from a doctor or psychotherapist if you continue to see these symptoms.

Repetitive Movements

Knowing what the body is trying to communicate can be challenging. You can help your child by recognizing behaviors that come out through repetitive movements. They might grimace, stretch their neck over and over, or crack their joints. Some lick their lips constantly, blink their eyes, and repeatedly clear their throat or make a distinct sound. These involuntary behaviors might be a sign of their stress—that is, they don't mean to start doing it; it just happens automatically.

We know you mean well when you encourage your child to stop; you may fear the behavior will never go away if you don't. But know that the child who bites their nails probably wants to stop, too. She can see that other people's nails look beautiful and neat. Her hands may hurt from nibbling or picking too much in some spots. She bites her nails automatically because her body is trying to manage inner worries. When your kid paces before a performance onstage and cracks her knuckles, it's tempting to say, "Stop it!" but the body is clever: even if you try to shut down that behavior, the worry will find another place to pop up until they have coping mechanisms in place to regulate their anxiety.

As one parent told us, "Oh, it was like Whac-A-Mole! Alba picked at her scalp. We finally got her to stop doing that because we explained to her that she'd get dandruff all over her shirt—and then she started picking her face and pulling out her eyebrows! And when that stopped, she was clenching her jaw! It was only then that we realized there must be some overall sense of anxiety that's driving all these behaviors."

Paying attention to your child's physical signs of worry will help you spot essential and helpful messages. Although not always, trouble settling the body can indicate something else is going on. Many parents are surprised to learn that symptoms of anxiety can have a great deal of overlap with physical health conditions or be an indication of neurodivergence.

For instance, 6-year-old Camila's parents were concerned about the tightness in her chest, difficulty breathing, and how tired she was all the time. After seeing their pediatrician, they discovered those reactions were also a result of asthma. If your child shows persistent symptoms we've talked about or suddenly develops new ones, seeing a doctor will help you illuminate what's going on and how you can help.

Anxiety in Other Forms

Often a parent will come to us with a tight facial expression or desperate sigh and say, "My kid's behaviors are out of control." But when we listen, we typically see the behavior or attitude for what it really is: anxiety. Worries come in many guises. Here are a few to be aware of.

Avoidance

Children who feel anxious about specific situations might avoid them to reduce their worry. They can beg you to sign them up for a coding group, then refuse to attend, yelling "I WON'T GO. NO WAY!" in the morning. Or they might react like 9-year-old James, who loved roller-coaster rides but whose body came to a halt while he was in line for one at the summer fair, even though his best friend said it was "the coolest!" James's dad was frustrated when he told us, "James talked incessantly about riding that damn thing for four weeks straight!" James, looking up, told his dad, "I really wanted to, but I can't now that I see it."

Kids sometimes avoid things not to upset you but to keep their worries at bay. They might refuse to go to school for days, and you later find out it's because they're afraid of confronting a particular classmate. They may avoid asking questions or seeking help in school for fear of embarrassment. Other kids may get quiet and getting them to go on adventures outside the home can be tricky. And you may be familiar with their long list of injuries or excuses to get out of any activity you want them to try.

Difficulty Separating

Oftentimes, avoidance and a need to be close to a parent go hand in hand. Some children have a hard time when a parent leaves their side (for school or bedtime) and worry that something terrible will happen to you while you're away. Eleven-year-old Lia needed constant reassurance that her dad would return, texting him five times per hour asking when his work dinner would be over.

Your child could always want you near them, especially if they are trying something new. Instead of enjoying their favorite game at a fun school event, they might cling to you despite having the opportunity to play. Some children might have a hard time tolerating you giving anything else your attention or being in a different room. They may experience jealousy or even anger when you spend time with others.

Sleep Difficulties

A few years ago, during a mindfulness presentation to a classroom of thirty-five third graders and their parents, we asked, "Who has trouble sleeping?" Almost everyone raised their hands, including the teachers. In a parenting workshop of two hundred people, we asked the same question and got the same response.

Children with worries especially have issues with bedtime. Sleep can be challenging for kids as it is their most extended separation from you—saying good night means hours away from you and alone, even if they share a bedroom with a sibling. These kids could wake up in the middle of the night and crawl into your bed regularly or struggle or stall to fall asleep because it means you will leave the room.

We know bedtime is often the most challenging part of your day. For a lot of kids, nighttime is also when their worries come out and they're ready to talk to you when all you want them to do is sleep. Children of all ages may not like the dark and get scared by the noises in the night. We also see night terrors or waking up super early or in the middle of the night. Parents usually mistake these antics for defiance, but in our offices, we recognize bedtime troubles as a sign that those pesky fears are getting kicked way up.

Reactivity

Wyatt worked really hard prepping his book report, but any time he stumbled over his words during practice, he'd lose his cool, yelling or throwing down his notes. His dad shared with us, "As parents, we'd talk between ourselves, wondering how we had brought up this angry 'jerk' who was disrespectful to us. We brought our kids up to have manners."

It often catches parents off guard when they find out that a kid's anger might be coming from a place of worry, not just bad behavior. After joining our group, Wyatt's dad had a lightbulb moment: Wyatt's outbursts were about his fear of messing up, not disrespect. That shift in perspective was a game changer.

We've talked about how anxiety can hijack the brain, kind of like when the Wi-Fi is down and your browser stops working temporarily. When this happens, kids might get noisy and lash out, or they might become withdrawn, offering little communication or frustrating "I don't know" responses when asked what's wrong. It takes time for their brains to reset after an anxiety spike.

Remember, kids aren't fully equipped to deal with stress and put their feelings into words—especially since the part of the brain that handles reasoning isn't fully grown. If your child reacts with anger or tears or goes silent, it's often anxiety in disguise. Handling these moments can be tough since it might feel like your kid is defying you. But keep in mind that their nervous system is just overloaded, and they're still learning to cope with that.

Rituals

If you notice your child needs to organize their belongings, straighten crooked items, or perform a particular routine in a specific order to feel OK or until it feels "just right," there could be significant underlying anxiety. For example, Hui's parents came to us concerned because their daughter needed to wash her hands and turn on and off the lights four times before she left the bathroom—and if anyone interrupted her, she would exclaim, "Don't interrupt me!" and have to begin again. Not everyone who follows a particular pattern or routine does so because of stress. But it gets into worrying territory if they become distraught, or even inconsolable, when they can't perform their ritual.

Similarly, your child might be repeatedly checking that the alarm was set before going to bed, scratching both arms to "make them even," or insisting that TV channels be only on odd numbers. This kind of anxiety makes them want to do things repeatedly or in a particular order, as their mind tries to manage the worry they feel on the inside by controlling what's happening in their environment. If you recognize your child in this description, be sure to get them evaluated for OCD.

Sliding Backward

Sometimes, children may temporarily return to earlier, more childlike behaviors or habits they had outgrown. They may bring Mr. Fluffles the teddy bear out from a storage bin or "forget" how to brush their teeth and ask you to do it. Regression is common throughout the course of a child's life, especially when they're learning something new or experiencing stress. This can catch parents off guard. Just when you think they've reached a secure stage, they might ask you to stay at basketball practice instead of running errands like you'd been doing, or they unexpectedly stop jumping off the diving board after they spent all last summer doing backflips. You might notice your child using baby talk or a change in their bedtime routines. If you're thinking, "Hey, my kid used to go to friends' houses to hang out, and now they need so much support or won't go," that's your signal that they might be experiencing anxiety.

Traumatic Stress

You may notice dissociation, which is how the mind escapes to manage overwhelming pressure, worry, or a traumatic event. Sometimes, it's mild, like spacing out briefly or daydreaming, or it can be more severe, where your child appears blank or might lose track of time or their sense of self for a while. It's like a mental escape where they might feel as if they're detached from themselves or from reality. It's typical for kids to have difficulty concentrating, and their attention spans are naturally short. Still, like anything else, if these things happen suddenly or occur more frequently, it may be a sign that they've experienced trauma. If you notice your child having recurring nightmares, flashbacks, or panic attacks about a specific incident they experienced in the past, this could indicate post-traumatic stress disorder (PTSD).

Big Warning Signs

The goal of this book is to coach you to stay calm as you help your kids navigate a world that can be chaotic, stressful, and confusing. We've said before that anxiety is part of growing up, but some expressions of worry require more immediate intervention.

Sometimes, parents mistake warning signs like kids running away from home or skipping class as acts of defiance, when they're signs that your child needs your support for deeper mental health concerns.

Self-Harm in All Its Dimensions

Kids under a lot of stress might try risky ways to cope with their pain, like using drugs or alcohol, having unprotected sex, or inflicting self-harm. Children can use household objects like pencil sharpeners, scissors, and razor blades to hurt themselves. Brooklyn told us, "I started cutting small lines on the inside of my thighs in fifth grade because I just wanted the bad feelings to disappear for even a few minutes. I knew it wasn't good for me even when I was doing it."

Look out for bruising, burning, pinching, or other injuries on the body, as they could be an indication of a child hurting themselves or that an adult is physically abusing them. Be sure to ask directly and lovingly about anything you see.

Here are some other stand-out signs that anxiety might have the upper hand with your child.

Suicidality

This is tough to think about, but it's not uncommon for kids, even at a young age, to have thoughts of not wanting to be alive. Recognizing and addressing these feelings in your child could be lifesaving. That's why it's crucial to be alert to the subtler signs, such as pulling away from others or talking like there's no hope, because these might mean your child is thinking about suicide and needs help immediately. Some children will say things like "I wish I wasn't here," or joke about suicide to cover up feelings of anguish. Ask them very calmly if they've thought about ending their life.

If they say they have, ask if they have a plan to kill themselves or whether they know how they would do it, and if the answer to either question is yes, treat it as urgent and call 911 or go to an emergency room. This advice isn't meant to alarm you, but to ensure you are equipped to keep your child safe. Meanwhile, secure any sharp objects and medications, and seek professional support. Above all, be available to listen. Talking about these feelings openly with you is a tremendous support—it doesn't make things worse.

Preoccupation with the Body, Food, and Exercise

If your child is really worried about their size or shape, that's often a sign they're feeling anxious and developing a poor body image. You might hear them talking about how bad they look or how they hate parts of their body. Sometimes, kids will start to obsess over calories or can't stop checking themselves out in the mirror or suddenly avoid certain activities, like swimming in public, because of body shame. Even at age 9, Tasmin did crunches before bed in secret because she was afraid of getting heavier. Dariush was similar when he was 10, lifting weights in his parents' in-home gym to get muscles because he wanted to look bigger.

You might also notice children developing strong preferences for what they can or cannot eat, or about texture, smell, and taste. They might avoid eating certain foods or entire food groups, and tell you they fear weight gain, feeling sick, or contamination. Others might try to find ways to curb their hunger without food. However, while the symptoms are food- and body-related, it is never really about the food.

To hide weight changes and eating behaviors, some kids might wear baggy clothes or cut food into tiny pieces or move it around the plate a lot. Savannah told us she would cough the food into her napkin to feed the dog later. Or they might eat a lot of food at once, like Carson, age 8, who told their mom, "Once I start eating, it feels like I can't stop." Some kids hide their behaviors because they know a parent won't approve, or because they don't want to experience embarrassment or humiliation. When Alice's mom discovered that her daughter was secretly taking laxative tea from the cupboard, Alice told her, "You drink it, too. I just want to be a little skinnier."

Sadly, kids in larger bodies are often praised for eating light, skipping meals, and eliminating food groups like carbohydrates. These are the very behaviors that landed 11-year-old Dima in inpatient treatment for an eating disorder: his parents missed his need for therapy because they thought he had a good reason for counting calories. These behaviors are not only problematic from a mental health perspective, but they can have a major impact on a child's growing body.

If you sense that these behaviors are becoming more extreme or intrusive, or you have noticed significant weight changes, have your child screened right away by a professional with training in eating disorders. Medical doctors without training might miss eating-disorder behavior, particularly in children with larger bodies.

Some children experience extreme distress because they feel they're in the wrong body or that they are not the gender they were assigned, which means they are transgender or nonbinary. They may have tendencies to restrict food or change eating and exercise habits in an effort to find relief. They may tell you directly that they want to get out of their body, numb it, not live in it, or change it to look more like the gender they are. Many will hesitate to share with you, so it's important to be on the lookout for these behaviors, especially during puberty. Be sure that any professional you consult is trans-affirming and specializes in gender dysphoria.

Why Seek Professional Therapy?

Parents often wonder if their child needs to "talk to someone." It's normal for all kids to show some anxious behaviors now and then—it's part of being human. However, if these behaviors become frequent or start impacting their overall well-being (e.g., they consistently avoid social interactions or have acute phobias about, say, leaving the house or being in enclosed spaces), it's time to seek advice from a social worker, school counselor, or child therapist. When getting your child screened, make sure to share any important behavior changes you've observed or written down.

Stress-driven behaviors might indicate an anxiety disorder. It's also common for a child to have more than one diagnosis at a time, like having anxiety along with depression, an eating disorder, or OCD. There is no shame in having a diagnosis; it can actually help create a map of how you and the people in your child's life can best support them, from finding the right therapists to getting proper accommodations at school and, if necessary, medication.

Whether or not your child receives a diagnosis, many of these behaviors can interfere with daily functioning and leave a child feeling distressed until they get proper guidance.

Remember, just because a child has anxiety now doesn't mean they always will, but without help, they could struggle significantly. Showing them now that there are tools and treatments to help their symptoms will put them on the road to caring for their mental health for the rest of their lives. That is one of the most valuable lessons you can impart to your children.

• • •

Now that you know what makes kids worry and how to spot it, it's time to look closer at the SAFER Parenting philosophy. Practicing SAFER Parenting requires intentional work, awareness, and patience; everything good does. As you read on, digest the lessons and tools we offer. Be an active reader: highlight sections, scribble notes, and discuss what you're learning with friends and family.

Some elements of SAFER Parenting may make you go, "I already do this." That's fantastic! There will also be parts that will be challenging to absorb because you will realize that you're doing something that inadvertently makes things less calm for your child. That's also a good thing. It means you are looking at yourself and growing. You are here learning for the benefit of both you and your family. We want you to give yourself a pass right now and say, "I'm doing things in a SAFER way starting today by becoming more informed, and that's a good start."

Most of all, be compassionate with yourself. Change doesn't happen overnight. Parents in our groups take time, sometimes over weeks, months, or even years, to integrate new methods into their parenting. Commit to try a little each day and practice one tool at a time. It will likely take several attempts before a new approach gets integrated. Slowly but surely, you will become a SAFER Parent who helps your child calm their worries.

Questions and Reflections
for Deeper Thinking

It's always a good time to take a breath. So, let's take one together before we delve into a few more prompts to help you reflect. In this chapter, we've explored how anxiety can manifest in unexpected ways in your child's behavior. The questions below will help you connect the dots between what you've learned and what you're observing at home—and in yourself. Take a moment to truly engage with these prompts, using them as a starting point for understanding and identifying your child's worries.

- What might your child be worried about, even if they haven't said it out loud? Have you noticed any new behaviors or physical complaints (e.g., nail biting, sleeplessness, headaches) that could signal worry?

- Does your child's way of expressing worry remind you of how you handle stress, either now or when you were a child?

- Are there recurring themes to your child's concerns? What settings and situations bring them out the most? Considering what you've learned, what might be important to talk over with a doctor or a therapist?

- Does your child avoid activities or struggle to interact with friends, attend events, or complete schoolwork? How long have you noticed this happening?

- What underlying feelings might be driving your child's more challenging behaviors? How can you maintain compassion in these moments?

Part II:
SAFER Parenting

• • •

Three

Set the Tone

Mom is at her computer when she hears her son crying, exactly as his friend chimes in with "But we didn't jump from that high in the tree!" Her son's wails grow louder as he rushes into the house with a bloody nose. Not knowing what happened, Mom flashes back to two years ago when he broke his arm. "Oh no-o-o," she thinks, and races through the house, shouting, "Honey! Honey! What happened? Is it your head, honey? Your arm again? Is something broken?!" Her volume alone makes the situation five times worse. A backyard fall is suddenly a full-on disaster.

Now imagine a different response. Mom is startled to see her son hurt, but she knows that someone needs to be in charge. She tells herself, "My anxiety is skyrocketing but panicking isn't going to help anyone." As she approaches her son, she repeats to herself, "I can handle this, I can handle this," and gently says, "It's OK, my love. I'm right here." Her son feels reassured seeing his mom navigate a confusing, scary situation. Crisis averted.

Leading with Calm

When your child faces intense emotions like fear or anxiety, your demeanor can either escalate or de-escalate these feelings. Young children, who are still learning to manage and articulate their emotions, look to you for guidance. Like young tiger cubs watching their parents for signals, your child is tracking you for cues. While parents don't mean to pass on their fears, stressed-out reactions inevitably lead children to absorb those feelings.

As you're discovering, the first and most effective way to help your child manage their emotions is by maintaining steadiness within yourself. This practice, widely known as co-regulation, allows you to share calm with your child, helping them feel at ease. Discovering and maintaining your own calm is a powerful tool for supporting your child's emotional regulation. By doing so, you can defuse tense situations and provide comfort—it's parenting magic! Your tranquility, much like a contagious yawn, influences your children, helping them find their own peace.

Maintaining composure is especially important in challenging or intimidating situations. Often, *the way* you communicate with your child matters more than the words themselves. By remaining grounded and even-keeled you provide a comforting presence that helps your children feel protected and at ease.

We know staying calm isn't easy, and it's only natural for your stress to get the best of you once in a while. But in this chapter, we'll explore ways to manage your stress and handle challenging moments with greater control and consistency. You'll learn to regulate your emotions as a practice, so you can navigate any situation and create a calmer environment for your child.

But first, let's discuss what prevents parents from maintaining a calm demeanor.

Roadblocks to Setting the Tone

In every chapter of this SAFER Parenting guide, we'll highlight the obstacles that might keep you from practicing a particular skill. This gives you a moment to reflect on any personal habits that might be obstructing your path. It's common to recognize yourself in these descriptions—we've seen these challenges affect thousands of parents. We're here to help you spot and understand these common pitfalls.

When it comes to staying calm, setting the right tone can be tough. Some parents react to intense moments with anger, others with sadness, others with anxiety. If you've run through all three of these emotions and it's still not time for breakfast, don't worry. Keep reading to learn how to recognize and manage whatever you're feeling inside.

Anger

Harper was 12 when she started therapy. Her dad said she seemed to worry about everything, from school and friendships to whether their dog got his yearly shots. But we found what she shared most intriguing: "Well, my dad always gets so mad if I just do something like spill my cereal, so I sort of always expect him to yell, which makes my hands shake when I'm pouring, even when he's not there."

We all get upset at times—that's just life—but when a parent regularly sets an angry or hostile tone in the home, children live in fear even when things are going OK. They tend to think negatively of themselves or assume they are the cause of whatever bad thing is happening. As Landon, age 8, told us, "If Mom's angry all the time and I can't get her to be calm or make her happy, I must be the problem."

Sometimes, anger feels like the best way to show your child you're serious. But while children may comply with strongly worded demands in the moment, they mostly end up terrified and their nervous systems suffer because of it. When a parent is yelling or acting in an angry way, a child goes into survival mode and their kid logic says, "I'm afraid she doesn't love me anymore. I don't want to lose my most important person." What looks like obedience is often a desperate attempt to stop you from being angry, because they want that feeling to go away as soon as possible.

We know that sometimes you can't help but yell, but kids don't learn in that fearful state, so anger ends up being unproductive and erodes their self-esteem. It's not just loud voices that kids pick up on. If you try to keep your feelings close to your chest but leave signs for your family to pick up on, the effects will be the same. "My mom always slams doors or says things under her breath when she's mad. She doesn't say she's mad, but we stay away because we know she is angry. It's scary," Naomi, age 10, told us. Learning to manage your frustration is challenging and takes time and effort. This is especially true if you grew up with parents who raged. If you're working on easing back on anger or hostility, here's what we recommend:

- Don't scream, use curse words, or call people names in front of your children.

- Avoid aggressive behaviors like yelling, threatening, giving the cold shoulder, or acting out angry feelings without calmly telling your child what you are mad about.

- Don't be rude to people you encounter, especially in front of your children—this also makes them nervous.

- If you find yourself acting out of anger and rage most of the time, seek a psychotherapist's support.

We know this is difficult. People don't wake up one day and stop being angry just because they read something in a book like this. At the same time, no parent we've ever worked with enjoys getting mad at their kids; it just happens. This is where parent coaching comes in. Many parents like you have committed to applying strategies that help them manage anger. With consistent practice, they can control their strong feelings most of the time.

Depression

Penelope, a mom of two, said in a parenting group one day, "I am so tired all the time. I get frustrated when the kids don't listen, which makes me feel even worse about myself. My eyelids feel heavy and I'm on the verge of tears every day."

Francesca, who is usually quiet, finds it hard to admit that when she's sad—which is often lately, since she had a miscarriage—she will react with "Do whatever you want," without really listening to what her kids are saying.

It's hard enough to take care of yourself when you're feeling depressed, let alone take care of your kids. But having depression does not make you a bad parent. It makes you human. In fact, striving to be present for your children while battling depression makes you a good parent, though it is by no means an easy task.

It's natural to feel sad, but we want you to notice when sadness becomes the overall tone at home. Everybody has times when they feel melancholy or have things they are grieving, some bigger and fresher than others. If a parent appears down all the time, a child can live with the sense that nothing is right in the world. They may feel confused and develop anxiety or depression themselves.

What's even scarier for a child is that they can't do anything to fix what's happening to their parent. Kelsey told us in a parenting group that her dad was so gloomy during her elementary school years that she spent most of her time tidying up corners of the house and organizing, hoping that a neater environment might make him happy.

Kids can be a great source of comfort and sometimes even offer wisdom, but it's important to know that children find it challenging when parents cry to them or lean on them for emotional support. Children can take those heavy emotions on as an insurmountable burden, thinking, "I can't make my parent feel better." Make it clear to your kids that you can handle your sadness, and that it is not their responsibility.

The Thin Line Between Caring and Over-Worrying

One day in a parenting session, Paula shared, "I worry about everything. 'Did I email the school? What's for dinner tomorrow? Was that cough serious?' I lose so much sleep that I'm irritable with the kids and end up running around frantically."

Another mom nodded and chimed in, saying, "My son came home upset because his teacher had been harsh. I immediately got worked up and said, 'What?! Should I call her? Can you do extra work?' It wasn't my best moment. He probably wished I'd just calm down."

You might find yourself stressed or anxious about the future—who isn't? But there's a thin line between being protective and over-worrying, and it's easy to cross. Over-worrying in front of the kids can make it seem like danger is always just around the corner, keeping everyone on edge.

In group, a mom shared, "My dad used to panic, cursing and scrambling for his keys. Now it's funny, but as a kid, it made every outing stressful." Some kids mimic this frantic energy. For instance, when a friend's birthday gift doesn't arrive on time, they might overreact: "The gift didn't come! This is the worst day ever!"

During a discussion on how children internalize stress, one dad was visibly upset, worried he'd harmed his kids. As someone who plans obsessively, he confessed, "I always worry about their future and second-guess every decision. They definitely pick up on my anxiety."

Anxiety is a natural part of life, but the way we handle it around our children can teach them either to stress about everything or to cope more calmly. Many of us were raised by worriers, too—it's easy to adopt our parents' habits. But you have the power to change the tone you set at home, helping your children learn healthier ways to handle life's uncertainties.

. . .

Anxiety and depression are real and sometimes arise without warning. If you feel sad or hopeless most of the time, it is essential to find a doctor or psychotherapist and seek medical help. If you notice you are having issues controlling your rage, sadness, or anxiety, and it is at the level where it's preventing you from participating in life because you are so overtaken by these feelings, talk to someone. Even when you feel like you are in a fog, a professional can help. If you have thoughts of hurting yourself, call the suicide hotline (988) to speak to somebody right away or go to the nearest emergency room. You can feel better.

Here are some parent coaching tools to help you set a calm tone even when you're feeling on edge.

Finding Peace in Anxious Situations

Much of the time, our emotional reactions are automatic. But as we've learned so far, as a parent, it's rarely helpful if you're the one having big feelings in front of your children: that's your kids' job. To curb your reactions, slow down and become aware of your typical patterns of behavior.

An exasperated mom with several young kids came to us

wondering: "How can I hold it together better when my nine-year-old accidentally spills her water bottle all over my laptop, like she did this morning? Gah!" We didn't say finding calm is easy—but know that it is always *possible*. Slowing down, breathing instead of exploding, scrunching a stress ball—you'll have plenty of tools in the emergency kit. When we asked the mom how she *wanted* to react to stressful situations with her children, her answer was simple and powerful: "I want to be the calm in the storm, not the storm in their calm."

Kids don't understand adult pressures and problems—all they know is that suddenly, something doesn't feel right. We're not saying that you must be completely fake and never show your feelings if you've had a terrible day, but try to collect yourself so you can set a calm tone. For example, try not to be cranky at your child's request for dessert because your boss yelled at you that day. Learning to choose a calm tone over an angry, detached, or worried one will not happen overnight, but with consistent and intentional practice, you will start to see change.

Identify What Sets You Off

We want you to take a second to get honest with yourself. Think about the last few days or the last week and ask yourself, "When did I lose my cool the most? What made me react?" Was it when your kids whined or didn't listen? When your partner remarked about the way you loaded the dishwasher? Did your in-laws push your buttons at dinner on Friday night? Or maybe something happened at work or with a friend? Sometimes, it's just the buildup of everything that makes you more on edge.

Next, think about how your body reacted to stress in those moments. What physical signals indicated you were emotionally upset? Did you feel your heartbeat pick up? Did your jaw clench? Perhaps your cheeks flushed or your shoulders tensed up to your ears. As much as you can remember, picture those physical reactions. Finally, recall how you behaved. Did you raise your voice at your kid? Did you snap back with sarcasm at your spouse? Did you give your family the silent treatment for twenty minutes?

By simply becoming aware of your reactions, you can meaningfully alter the course of critical moments. Slowing down and intentionally changing your gut responses can completely transform a situation. (Never fear, we'll address children's unproductive, anxiety-inducing behaviors and how to assist in modifying them later. But for now, we are starting with you.)

Hit Pause

Any time you're starting to feel angry, anxious, or upset and are about to react to your child (or partner or in-laws, for that matter), do whatever you can to take a moment before saying or doing anything. The best way to do that is to notice the impulse as it arises and stop your reaction in its tracks. Try to identify the feeling or pinpoint the places in your body where you're holding the stress: "I'm driving to my son's school to drop off the homework he forgot to bring with him, and now I'm late for work. I am so overwhelmed and angry. I feel it in my chest. I want to cry."

Next, remind yourself of your goal: "As a parent I want to be there for my child even when they mess up. I can't be a support if I'm this upset." By pausing and naming your feelings, you give yourself a chance to access a calmer state and make a different choice.

Research suggests that labeling emotions, even in your head, activates the brain region associated with reason and logic, and lessens activity in the amygdala, the danger alarm system of the brain. Instead of experiencing a vague or overwhelming sense of unease, naming feelings helps the rational decision-making part of the brain to start working again, which makes the uncomfortable feelings start to become more manageable.

Recover Your Calm

To learn how to bring your calm back, use these techniques we've implemented with clients over the years. These skills activate the body's relaxation response so you can gain more control over how you respond to your children. Like with forming any other habit, you want to try using these skills regularly, and the more you try them, the better they will work.

• *Get Your Feelings Out*
Write your feelings down in a journal (even if it's one sentence a day). Call or text a friend and share with them. Seriously, it helps!

• *Take a Break*
Spend a little extra "me time" in a warm bath or shower. Get exercise or stretch in your living room. Listen to calming music (or heavy metal, if that's your balm), tend to plants, wash the dishes, solve a sudoku puzzle, or do a calming craft activity. Stay off

your phone and find something else to access joy that brings you back to . . . you.

If you're feeling lethargic or emotionally low and can't get a moment of peace, say to your child: "I'm feeling down in the dumps today. It's not about you, and it's going to be OK." Giving voice to your present state in these situations goes a long way. Include them in a relaxing activity: "How about we do something more mellow together, like a puzzle?" Or maybe take ten minutes to find animal shapes in the clouds together.

• Do a Sensations Inventory

Direct your attention to as many of your five senses as you can. Open a window and listen to the sounds you hear outside. Take a whiff of your morning coffee beans. Close your eyes and feel the tiny curves of your kid's noodle art from kindergarten. Using your senses and describing them anchors you in the present moment, reducing internal agitation and fostering a sense of composure. Again, if your child needs you right away, do the exercise right in front of them—or invite them to name what they're sensing along with you.

• Hold That Thought

Take a break when an argument is brewing. If you feel the urge to continue talking in a tense moment, say to your family member, "Let's pause and finish this later when we both feel more settled." You might even forget about the tiff by tomorrow.

• Breathe

Thousands of studies have shown the significant impact of deep inhalation and exhalation on the nervous system. Changing the pace of your breathing slows your heart rate and activates the parasympathetic nervous system, or the mechanism that helps relax your body after danger or times of stress.

Parents we coach often start off saying, "This breath control stuff doesn't work for me"—until they've tried it a few times in action. There is no better way to believe this than to give it a whirl yourself. One breath could be the difference between a negative interaction with your child and a positive one.

Take a few deep breaths when you feel overwhelmed, or try a small but mighty exercise called 4-7-8:

1. Inhale slowly for a count of four.

2. Hold that breath as you count to seven in your head.

3. Exhale for a count of eight. Do a few rounds anytime, anywhere!

• *Get Grounded Like a Mountain*

We know it's hard to feel calm when you're angry or scared, so imagine yourself as a mountain. Really imagine it! You are a beautiful, vast mountain with a massive, unwavering base and a towering peak reaching into the clouds. Like a mountain, you are composed and unshakeable, remaining steady against the endlessly changing background of wind, water, and sky. The sun and moon dance above you, reminding you that each night gives way to a new day. Imagine your child taking refuge here, under one of your trees, feeling safe from strong winds and torrential rain. You are that mountain, and when you embody that grand stillness in the face of challenges, you set a calm tone.

If you feel a reaction coming, sit still and take a deep breath.

Tell yourself, "I am a strong mountain for my child." As you exhale, imagine your head being high as a peak, your arms as the sides of the mountain, and your legs as its expansive base. Repeat this and see how many mountain breaths you need to feel grounded.

You don't have to fully believe this exercise works to use it. Fake it until you make it, because each time you try it, you'll get closer to being steady like that mountain. Say it with us: *I am a big, majestic mountain, and my emotions do not knock me over. Seasons may come and go, but I will remain a calm and enduring presence for my child.*

One of the most iconic reactions we've ever gotten was from Bianca, a mom who was admittedly far away from having a routine to get calm. She said, "When you told me to get grounded like a mountain, I thought, 'Get grounded like *what*? Where did I find these yo-yos?'" But her go-to reactions, she admitted, were anger and frustration. We observed that she was quickly overwhelmed, especially when under a deadline or overly tired.

"Growing up," she said, "no one in my family talked about calming down. I was born and raised in NYC, and we're Italian. We move fast and scream more than we speak. I could only imagine what my sisters would say if they saw me doing parent coaching." She'd been doing great at stopping her go-to reactions, she said, until last week, when she was on a deadline and working from home.

"I lost it on my kids when they knocked on my door," she told us. "I yelled, 'I am *on the phone*! Are you kidding me! Get out of here, how many times do I have to tell you this?'"

We all sat there for a minute. "I know," she sighed. "I didn't Set the Tone there or pause—I was more like a wild storm. Later, things turned around when my middle schooler couldn't finish her humanities project. She started stressing big-time. She even mentioned college applications, and she's in sixth grade. I caught her teary-eyed, sniffling, and ripping up her work into little pieces the night before it was due! She had so many worries, and the thought that I might have caused them left me devastated. Reflecting on it now, I understand that this instant guilt often leads me to snap at the people around me."

It's not easy to recognize the things that get in the way of calm, so we were excited about Bianca's newfound awareness.

She then said, "I was just about to lose it when I saw that stupid mountain in my mind. It gave me an instant chuckle and reminded me to slow down. I took a breath like you told me to. I didn't yell at her. I said to myself, 'I'm about to kick my kid out to Mars.'" (It goes without saying she doesn't kick her children, ever. She's just naming her feelings and thoughts and being honest with herself.)

"Then I asked, 'How can I help?'"

She went on to tell the group, "I feel so ridiculous saying it, but it worked. There were no more tears, and we got to bed at a decent hour. We made a plan that evening. She got up early in the morning to finish her work, and I even had time to look at it before we left for school. I won't lie; I had to drag my body out of bed that morning. She looked exhausted, too, the poor thing. I see it clearly now. My yelling makes it worse."

So, give it a try! We love a practice that doesn't take equipment or much time.

· *Store Up Calm*

It's helpful to keep in mind that regularly "storing up calm" can substantially lower your baseline levels of irritation or worry. Create a small routine that helps you find calm, whether that's taking a short walk first thing in the morning or reading a few pages of a book before the kids are up. It's challenging because you're pulled in so many directions as a parent, but it's still essential to regularly take care of your nervous system. Knowing we recommend this might help offset your guilt for taking time for yourself. Start with a few minutes each day and try something out until you find what works for you. Try your hardest to carve out time, even if it's five deep breaths a day.

Safe vs. Scary Framing

Especially around children, it's necessary to talk about our concerns in a way that maintains a positive and non-fearful outlook. As you're seeing in this chapter, your emotional state can significantly influence those around you. When you express anxiety about something, it can also make your child feel uneasy. It's important to be mindful of how you talk about your fears. Let's look at a real-life example to illustrate this:

During one of our sessions, a dad shared a telling moment: "My wife really dislikes crowds and makes it known. 'You could get sick from someone sneezing close to you. There are pickpockets.' Stuff like that. It's no surprise our son now refuses to go to crowded places with us." Their son Leon was already dragging his feet about attending a summer concert for which the family had bought tickets months in advance.

The son was reacting to what we call *scary framing*—portraying a situation as if danger is imminent. For instance, if you're driving and yell, "Whoa there, that car almost caused an accident! We could have been seriously hurt!" As much as you can, try to use *safe framing* instead. In this case, you would rephrase more neutrally, "That was close! That driver wasn't paying attention."

Here are some examples to help you differentiate between scary framing and safer, more positive framing:

Scary framing: "Being out after dark is risky. Just one wrong look and you could be in serious trouble. Pedestrian accidents are frighteningly common at night."

Safe framing: "It's safer to be home before dark. However, if you need to be out later, keep your phone handy and stay alert. Being visible and aware are your best precautions after sunset."

• • •

Scary framing: "There was a fire nearby recently. It's terrifying to think about what could have burned down. I've heard of families losing everything."

Safe framing: "There was a fire close by, but the firefighters were quick to respond. It's good to know we have such reliable services."

• • •

Scary framing: "Mom's job loss is a huge blow. We're all worried about finances and whether we can afford any summer trips."

Safe framing: "Mom has been let go, but she's already getting support from friends and looking into new opportunities. We're handling things as a team."

How to Have Conversations About Difficult Topics

It's hard to go even one day without bumping into a topic or experience that's difficult to explain to your kids. Your 11-year-old might end up in tears after accidentally clicking on a video about a school shooting. Meanwhile, the TV at Grandma's house blares news of a perceived nuclear threat, with a noticeably concerned reporter. An old family friend, visibly ill and pale from cancer, might visit your house.

No matter how tough the topic, you want your children to feel like they can come to you to talk about it. When they hear you say, "I am always here to listen to anything on your mind. You are never in trouble for sharing with me," your children will be more likely to bring you what troubles them most. If they come to you, it's important that you don't flinch when they ask you about pornography, drinking, drugs, or any other topic. Your words and demeanor should reassure them, "You have a safe place here with me to talk when it's scary out there."

Travis asked us one night, "But what if it's an ongoing issue like fentanyl or teen suicide? How do I know what to tell them and when? I don't want my children to learn about things too young." Here's the hard truth: if you don't tell them, someone else will.

Let's look at five steps to help make having tough conversations with your child easier.

Step 1: *Plan Ahead and Get Calm*

Practice what you want to say with another adult so that when you're saying it to your child, it isn't the first time. Even say it in the mirror. This is especially useful when it's a topic that makes you uneasy. Take a stroll, vent to a friend, and don't forget about your breath—it's always there to steady you.

If you can, pick a setting that puts you at ease so you can be as composed as possible. When we ask parents to get calm before broaching a tough subject with their kids, they often ask us, "But what if I don't feel calm? This is very hard news to share." Remember, it helps kids feel safe if you speak with a warm confidence that communicates that you are not panicked about what's happening, no matter how frightening the message you must deliver might be.

Choose a time during the day to talk. Children need space to ask questions and digest complex information. The truth is, we adults do, too. Life can get in the way of finding the ideal moment. As best you can, try to avoid having hard conversations before bed or school because it can cause them to have difficulty sleeping or feel extra distracted in class.

When all else fails, be like a duck: calm on the surface even though you're paddling away underwater.

Step 2: *Share Facts and Ask Questions*

Kwame told us in session one night, "Ashley and Maria, my daughter never fails to bring up intense questions that catch me off guard! She'll ask about war or why people bully one another. Last week, she asked me about home invasions because she heard about one from a friend at pottery class. Half the time, I have no idea what to say."

Here's a gentle way to approach such a scenario:

- State the facts clearly and avoid sharing too many details. Be age-appropriate, being careful not to burden your child. This means modifying the information and complexity of what you tell them to fit their age and ability to understand. If you're telling them about a time your wallet was stolen when you were younger, leave out the more intense details, such as the fact that the thief had a gun.

- Opt for examples from everyday experiences they can relate to. When discussing a family member in the hospital with a younger child, explain, "The doctor is going to fix something inside their body, like when we fixed your broken bicycle chain."

- Project calm and evenness rather than anxiety. Leave out how stressed you are. Otherwise, kids can get even more concerned and feel they must care for you or bottle up their fear.

- Stick to one topic per conversation so you don't overwhelm your child. Talking about drugs is challenging enough without getting into climate change and puberty.

With any topic, start by saying, "I'm glad you're asking me about that. We can certainly talk about it." Ask them what they know and feel about what's going on with simple questions, like "Can you share with me what you know?" Debunk incorrect information and ask questions slowly, giving them time to answer. Be OK if they don't have much to say. You might ask, "What are your friends saying about it? Or your teachers?" It is always a good idea to ask, "Is there anything you're confused about?" Open the door to a conversation and allow them to ask questions: "Do you have any questions for me? You can ask now or any time later."

If you don't have an answer to a difficult question or aren't sure how much information to give on the spot, say, "Good question. Let me look into it and get back to you on that one." Take a break to research information, get advice, talk it out with another adult, and follow up with your child. You should also check back a few days later by asking, "Hey, did you have anything more you wanted to ask me?" Don't pressure yourself to have all the answers in the moment.

Step 3: *Make Space for Feelings*

Along the way, be sensitive to your child's emotions and notice how they respond. Pay attention to their expressions and body language. Do they look glum? Are they tapping their feet nervously? If they seem upset at any point, pause and say, "This is hard, let's take a break. I'm right here." For some kids, these conversations will make them anxious, and you'll notice they may start to panic. Use a calming tool from the following chapter that your child likes most.

Provide the space for children to share their emotions. Ask, "How do you feel? Do you have any worries about this?" Then listen and don't correct what they say. If they say, "That sounds so scary," or "It makes me nervous," let them know it's OK to feel that way. Children need to hear, "Being scared is OK." But always cap that thought with "I got you."

Keep in mind that not all children will worry, and they don't necessarily have the same fears as adults. Don't be offended at their seeming lack of compassion toward world events in the form of an outburst, a joke, or going quiet. One dad we know was seriously anxious about explaining the Holocaust to his 10-year-old, who asked about the word after seeing it in a children's book on Albert Einstein. The dad took a breath as they read together the section that gave an age-appropriate overview of the atrocities of World War II. Rather than asking follow-up questions about the millions killed, his son looked up in wonder and said, "Daddy, I had no idea 'World War II' needs Roman numerals!"

Sometimes, difficult information is too much for young nervous systems to handle.

Step 4: *Lean Into Safety*

Help your child identify teachers, school administrators, and other trusted adults who are there for them. Focus on all the people and structures in place that work to keep them out of harm's way.

Name the facts and educate your child about realistic dangers while focusing on what you, as their parent, can do to keep them safe. Eight-year-old Victoria was anxious about being wrongfully blamed for a symbol drawn in the school bathroom. She asked her mother, "What if they think I did it because I'm brown? They're so racist. What if I get expelled?" Her mother responded, "It would be completely unfair to be wrongly accused. If that ever happens, have the front office call me immediately. I'll come and discuss this with the principal." Relieved, Victoria said, "You would? OK, that makes me feel better." Her mom affirmed, "Absolutely! I'll always have your back."

When possible, give children a plan for staying safe. Don't lie to make them feel better; let them know what they will experience. Before getting on a plane, your child might say, "I'm so scared we will have to land in the ocean." Here's how you might respond: "It's doubtful that it'll happen, but if there are any problems, oxygen masks will come down, and I'll put one right on you. We'll each put on a life vest, and the flight attendants and the pilot will tell us what to do each step of the way." Next, remind them how to calm themselves on the plane. Speak warmly and confidently, showing that you believe in the safety measures you identified.

Step 5: *Give Your Child Something to Do*

Children need a sense of control when things feel overwhelming, so they often feel better when they know they can take action.

For example, teaching children how to keep their hands clean and why we may want to wear a mask when we are sick gives them something to do to manage their own safety. Having a volunteer project to focus on helped Diya, age 7, with her sadness when people set up and lived in tents on the streets outside her building. Dad said, "She couldn't walk by without bursting into tears. I really understood her pain. Now, she creates care kits for unhoused people and has even started making her own soaps. It's turned into a real passion for her."

Your child's mind might find a creative way to feel safe even in the most frightening scenarios. If a child knows the procedure for an active shooter drill and says something like "If we shut the blinds, then they definitely can't get to us," you don't have to correct them; instead, share that you understand they have those safety measures. You could say, "Keeping the blinds closed if there ever is a shooter will help keep you safer!" From there, you can ask, "What else can you do to stay safe at school?" Heartbreakingly, we know the blinds are not guaranteed to keep an intruder out, but it's not useful to fact-check or correct them in those moments.

Sometimes, children will share their fantasies about a better outcome of a prior stress-inducing event as a way to process and manage their emotions. After a school shooting in a third-grade classroom, the survivors drew pictures of the attacker encountering slime outside the gates, slipping and falling before ever reaching the school doors. This was an earnest way to help themselves feel calmer. Your child's fantasies may be unrealistic, and that's OK. They might return to the idea in their mind several times more to help soothe worries.

Teach your children essential skills for protecting themselves. Discuss what to do if someone tries to get them in their car or touches them inappropriately. Empower them to practice saying no, loudly and powerfully, in threatening situations.

Tell them, "If somebody threatens to hurt you, have a trusted adult nearby call me immediately." Ask them to memorize your number.

These strategies pave the way for more challenging discussions. Always find your calm first. Then, share facts with your child, ask questions, and allow them to express their feelings, encouraging them to turn to you when they're confused or troubled. Explore Chapter 4 to learn in-depth skills to validate your child's feelings. Using this approach eases anxiety—for both you and your child—during and after these conversations.

When explaining complex issues to children, like the concept of death, it's essential to use age-appropriate examples they can understand. Consider a conversation where a mom carefully explains the death of a schoolteacher to her son, using a SAFER approach:

Mom: "Sweetheart, I need to share something important with you. It's something the school will talk about tomorrow, but I wanted us to discuss it first. Ms. Patel, a first-grade teacher at your school, has died. She had a heart attack. Do you remember when we talked about how when a flower or a bug dies, it doesn't come back?"

Son: "Yes."

Mom: "It's similar with people. Death is a difficult and sad part of life, and it's OK to feel upset about it. Just like plants and bugs, people have their life cycle, too."

Allow your child to ask questions:

Son: "What's a heart attack?"

Mom: "A heart attack happens when someone's heart has a big problem. It doesn't usually happen to people when they are young, and we take care of our hearts by eating healthy foods and exercising."

Son: "That's scary! Does that mean you and Daddy will die, too?"

Mom: "Eventually, everyone dies, but Daddy and I are doing everything we can to stay healthy and be here with you for a very long time. We love you so much!"

Encourage them to share their emotions:

Mom: "How are you feeling, love?"

Son: "I'm sad about Ms. Patel's daughter. She's in fifth grade."

Mom: "It is very sad, and I'm here to talk all about it. You know what? Feeling sad means you have a kind heart. I know sometimes when you feel this way you like to draw. I'll grab your paper and markers."

Son: "Yeah. Will you sit with me?"

Mom: "Absolutely I will. What do you think of also making a card for Ms. Patel's family? It will show them how much you care."

Son: "I know, I'm going to draw them my favorite dinosaur."

End the conversation by reassuring them of their safety and your availability:

Mom: "It's a lot to think about, and it's OK to have more questions later. If you do, you can always talk to me. You can share your feelings and get a hug any time you need it."

Through this dialogue, Mom provided information in a way her son could understand and validated his feelings. The child cried for a while after he made the card, but they snuggled extra long before bed that night, and Mom made sure to follow up after school the next day.

Elements of a Calm Environment

As a parent, setting the tone involves being mindful of the environment around your child. This section offers guidance on enhancing your home life and daily routine. Understandably, certain family situations may prevent you from applying these suggestions, no matter how badly you want to. If some recommendations seem unrealistic for you and your child, be gentle with yourself and do your best. Your child already has you—a loving parent determined to learn from this book and provide support, which is fundamentally what they need most. Incorporate all or as many of these elements as you can.

First, Do Nothing

Imagine this scene: It's late afternoon, and "Daddy" Sam is tinkering with the toilet because it's been making noise for the last week. The dog, Dennis, lies snoozing, only opening one eye to see who gives him a quick snuggle or pat on the head as they pass his bed in the living room. "Dad" Jo makes meatballs for Saturday night spaghetti dinner while Charlotte, age 8, walks around and eyes the toy closet. She hasn't played with her Hula-Hoop in months, and she pulls it out. Kevin, their youngest, is heard whining, "Dad, I don't know what to do, I'm bored," as he plops down at the table and begins coloring. Jo says, "Well, let's see how far that takes you. What will you color today?" The house is busy but calm, and everyone entertains themselves.

Children need this kind of free, unstructured time, also called "free play," to allow their nervous systems to rest and restore, and to learn how to occupy themselves in quiet moments. When free play is over, try to maintain this unhurried pace as much as possible, especially when leaving the house. Leave cushion time in between activities, allowing extra room for children to transition from one place to another to help reduce anxiety in day-to-day life.

Make Home More Fun

Kids spend all day at school, sometimes heading straight into after-school activities followed by homework well into the night. When they come home, greet them with excitement. Playing games and having spontaneous fun is a potent antidote to our biggest worries. Surprise them with an impromptu obstacle course or karaoke contest. Have a night where you do everything with your left hand (if you're all righties). Turn delivery boxes into a robot costume that your kid can wear around the house. And be sure to infuse humor and lightheartedness into every day. There are plenty of other times to be serious. Childhood only happens once.

Keep Things Age-Appropriate

Nine-year-old Dillon was suddenly getting back in bed with his dad, who was concerned. In our session, Dillon's dad casually mentioned that the boys had downed Sweet Tarts and watched *Harry Potter* together when his older son came home from college. He was so happy they were bonding, but our ears perked up. "How many have they watched?" we asked. As we feared, they had marathoned the entire film series, which was when Dillon started having problems sleeping. Dad said, "He read all the books practically without looking up and was totally fine reading about the creepy Dementors that feed on happiness, so I had no reason to think the movies would be a problem. But he keeps going on about Voldemort's snake attacking one of the Weasley characters. I thought it was all the candy, to be quite honest."

Creating a safe home means ensuring that your child is not exposed to content they may not be ready for. Delete text conversations your children could discover on your phone that are not meant for their eyes. We suggest waiting until your children have gone to bed to watch movies or shows with adult themes. If you watch while they're still awake, consider wearing earbuds. Be careful about access to news and podcasts with adult content, and don't share troubling facts about world events without context, like "Wow, fifty thousand people died in that earthquake!"

Pay close attention to what your child does online. The longer you can wait to give your child access to social media, the better. Install parental controls that allow you to track their safety while they learn the critical skills of being online, such as what not to write or post and how to identify when they should block someone's account. Monitor what they watch: while it may be endearing that they are watching the social media channel of a child just two years older than them, keep in mind that the age gap is relatively large, and they could be exposed to concepts they are not yet ready for. They could also encounter risky advice from influencers who lack formal training. Get over-involved to ensure their engagement remains age-appropriate and safe.

Avoid creating a home centered around electronics where everyone is constantly on devices. Have No-Tech Tuesdays or set up a basket by your door where everyone stashes their devices during certain set hours. Make off-screen activities a priority for everyone.

Establish Consistency

Predictability is an important way to set a secure tone in your home. When children have routines they can count on, it helps them to feel settled in what they know is ahead instead of worrying about what might happen next.

Think back to your childhood school schedule: the days were structured, the bells rang at the same time each day, and recess and lunch were almost always at the same time. For some kids, school is the most stable thing they can rely on when their home is unpredictable, and you can imagine how knowing that the teachers, classmates, and routines will be the same every day can be comforting to them. This predictability helps their nervous systems to relax so they can be present to learn.

Some families have a specific night when they watch a movie together. Valentina, age 10, told her uncle, "Knowing what's happening on the weekends helps me not worry so much. My family does game night most Saturday nights, and every Sunday my cousins come over."

For kids with two homes, make sure they know where they're going and on which days as much as possible. Place a calendar on the refrigerator and include after-school activities and any set plans for the weekend. Seeing the week's activities helps them feel more prepared and in control, which reduces stress and worry. Use an app or a shared electronic calendar for co-parents to stay up-to-date with appointments and events.

You can't always help when something changes but try not to switch the routines on your children at the last minute unless you absolutely can't help it. Being left to wait is annoying to adults but worrisome for children, so be sure to pick up your kids when you say you will or let them know you will be late.

It may be hard for you to have a steady after-school schedule—it doesn't work for every family—but consider where else you can create consistency. For example, Caleb expects to get chicken fingers and chocolate pudding in his lunch box on Tuesdays. For Kayla, her dad gets home right around bedtime, and she knows that no matter what, he'll come in and give her a kiss on her forehead.

That said, make sure the routines in your home are adaptable enough to adjust to unexpected events or changes. A rigid, unmovable schedule can also create distress for children.

Parenting on the Same Page

Another important way to bring a sense of ease is for parents to align their outlook and rules at home. When parents have different parenting philosophies, it causes children to question whether they should follow one or the other, making them feel confused and overwhelmed.

Jade and Kyle were raised in vastly different households— she had a strict family, while he grew up with few rules. After having children, they each followed the parenting model they'd grown up with. Mom insisted that homework should be done right when the kids got home, whereas Dad would say, "Who cares about homework! It's elementary school." He was a self-described pushover for his girls: "It doesn't matter what they ask, I can't say no." When they started working with us, the children were 6 and 9 years old, and both kids were showing signs of worry. The teacher of the youngest child had just emailed to say that she was having some behavioral issues at school. Mom explained, "I tell my kids *no* when it's a no, but he's the fun parent, causing us so many problems at home. He never backs me up when I say no to the kids. They can tell I'm shooting eye daggers at him, and I know the kids feel the tension."

We know you won't always agree with your co-parent, but it's important to work on getting on the same page. Here are some simple tips for how to navigate this situation:

- In front of the kids, if one parent says no, back them up as much as possible to avoid sending mixed messages.

- Maintain respect and civility between adults by using kind language with one another.

- Work out your differences of opinion when your children are out of the house or you are sure they're asleep (children listen behind closed doors).

- As much as possible, decide on rules and consequences ahead of time with your co-parent.

Prioritize Your Child's Sleep

You know how much more agitated and grumpy you feel when you don't sleep. Kids are the same. When children are tired, they can be more irritable and hyperactive and have difficulty throughout their day, and worry tends to rise at night. Make your child's sleeping environment comfy and be consistent with bedtimes and waking times. Dim the lights to signal that it's time to wind down and speak in lower tones to set the mood for sleep, even if the adults are staying awake.

Instill a routine to help bring calm. Play meditative whale sounds or relaxing cello music as the lights go out. Snuggle and read a few pages of a book together. You can recap the day's highlights and offer warmth and love by stroking their hair. Create a habit, but, as we said, don't get so set in it that altering it becomes too difficult. You don't want to find yourself in a nightly bedtime circus, forced to scratch out the entire alphabet on their backs and entertain them with shadow puppets, else they refuse to even shut their eyes.

If your children go to bed independently, share two things you love about each other or three things that you are grateful for each day, or do a handshake sequence that you two invented to say good night. Some kids may want to listen to part of a podcast or write in a journal. Sean and his mom decided that now that he's 8 and can go to bed on his own, he and his mom say, "I love you the most," to say good night.

Routines change as children get older: maintain no screens for at least an hour before bedtime. We love things like lavender sprays or a special blanket (perhaps even a weighted blanket) to create a cozy atmosphere—and remember, no one is too old for a stuffed animal!

. . .

We're all human, which is why expecting to maintain perfect calm all the time is like aiming for the stars with a slingshot—admirable, yes, but give yourself a break! Setting the tone is a gradual process. Begin today by identifying your roadblocks and committing to a calming tool the next time something rattles you. Practice the new approaches you're learning—refining your language for difficult topics in front of a mirror or rehearsing with a friend—and focus on reframing your thoughts and words in safe versus scary ways. Try to embrace the challenges and turn them into victories, one calm interaction at a time!

Questions and Reflections
for Deeper Thinking

Before we move on, take a few minutes to think about the insights that emerged for you in this chapter. How you manage worry in your life can reveal a great deal about your childhood as well as the emotional climate you're creating for your own children. By examining these connections, you can identify where you might improve your reactions and create a more supportive, calm environment for your children. Here's what we're wondering:

- What was the general atmosphere in your house while you were growing up? Did your parents or caregivers often seem angry, sad, or anxious?

- How do the people in your household today, both adults and children, impact your ability to Set the Tone? Which behaviors challenge your ability to stay calm?

- Be honest with yourself—are there specific reactions or behaviors you need to keep in check around your kids? Overall, how would you say your moods affect them and other people around you?

- What steps can you take to create a more calming and consistent environment at home? How can you introduce more fun and play into your child's life?

- What kind of daily routine could you establish that brings you calm? Are there tasks you could delegate or seek help with to reduce your stress level?

Four

Allow Feelings
to Guide Behaviors

Picture the typical morning madness at the Rosales house: Gabriella, age 11, a diligent student and the captain of her soccer team, is frantically searching for her cleats. She knows the importance of punctuality, not just for school, but especially for her team practices. Her anxiety spikes as the minutes tick by, and it doesn't help that her younger brother is leisurely finishing his breakfast, seemingly oblivious to the stress building around him. The second she finds her shoes, Gabriella turns to her brother. "Let's go, stupid idiot. Finish!" Which only makes him slow down and pour more Crunch Berries into his bowl.

Gabriella's mother knows she has a choice in how to react. She could scream at both kids, as in "That's it, you two! I've had enough! Both of you, get your shoes on. We're leaving right now!" Or . . . she could take an extra minute and be the voice of grown-up reason. Fortunately, Mom goes for option number two: "I know being late stresses you out. It's OK to be anxious. It's not OK to insult your brother. As for you, Cap'n Crunch, please finish up and put your bowl in the sink. We're leaving in three minutes."

Sometimes, parenting feels like you're starring in your own version of one of those adrenaline-fueled TV shows or high-stakes action films. Every move demands precision, and you're constantly on your toes, racing to stay ahead before it all unravels. And when things start to fall apart, it's often because you're up against unpredictable forces—like children's big feelings.

When parents implement the coping tools for kids discussed in this chapter, life doesn't have to be a disaster movie. Read on to build the necessary skills to take on whatever Hollywood-worthy kid crisis comes your way, even if it's just a meltdown at the breakfast table. We'll teach you how to support your child in regulating their emotions, guide them toward effective coping strategies, and avoid unhelpful behaviors.

Why Emotional Regulation Matters

There is a saying by Jon Kabat-Zinn that goes, "You can't stop the waves, but you can learn to surf." In the same way, you can teach your child coping skills that help them "ride out" their emotional ups and downs with a little more finesse. This is the hallmark of emotional regulation, that ability to manage strong feelings like worry, frustration, excitement, anger, or embarrassment.

Imagine your child is in high school, collaborating on a group project, when a teammate gives feedback that stings. How should they react? One option could be to retaliate, saying, "What's your problem? I do more work than any of you!" and storm out of the room. Alternatively, they might internalize the critique, thinking, "Everyone must dislike me; I'm sure I'm gonna fail."

However, with the right emotional regulation skills—skills you can model and help them develop—your child could handle this differently. They might pause and think, "Being called out is frustrating, but I'll take a moment to cool down and address this later."

Teaching children to recognize and manage their emotions allows them to respond more constructively. For instance, rather than acting out their frustration by hiding their sister's favorite toy, they learn to articulate their feelings. They can acknowledge, "I'm annoyed," or realize, "I feel scared. I need to ask for help." This self-awareness is the first step in handling their emotions responsibly.

Children who can identify, express, and manage their feelings are better equipped to handle stress, build strong relationships, and achieve academic success. Their enhanced emotional regulation not only boosts self-esteem but also helps them resist peer pressure and reduce anxiety, fostering long-term mental well-being.

When Emotions Are Dismissed, Behaviors Get Worse

In our years working with kids and parents, we've discovered that children with a working knowledge of their emotions can better navigate life. Therefore, children need to be encouraged to recognize, understand, and express their feelings instead of suppressing them. A child without good coping tools means worry is growing inside, which leads to more negative behavior on the outside in what becomes a never-ending cycle. You may see your child pushing back on boundaries and hurting others or themselves. For instance, they might slam the door in your face when you say no to the fifteenth request for an expensive device they want because, well, *"Everyone else has it!"* Intense anger has taken control; this child, like all children, needs tools to regulate and manage emotions.

Your child's more challenging behaviors are often distress signals for help. Often, there's a good chance they don't know how to manage their feelings yet. Listening to your child whine, cry, scream, or talk back can be aggravating and exhausting, no doubt. We want you to go from thinking, "My child is acting badly," to "My child needs my assistance badly." Children don't just wake up one day and say, "From now on, I won't throw a tantrum that's out of proportion to the situation." It's your job to teach them how to manage those big feelings by allowing them to feel them in the first place. Over time, as kids get to practice, they learn to emotionally regulate.

Your Golden Rule: Guide the Behavior, Not the Feeling

Allow your child's feelings to be there and guide them away from unhelpful behaviors and toward productive coping skills. Say it with us: "All feelings are welcome, always. Behaviors are what I will guide." Don't teach kids to stop having emotions.

We'll cover how to deal with your child's unproductive behaviors in a minute, but first let's look at what can trip parents up when it comes to accepting feelings in real time.

Roadblocks to Allowing Feelings to Guide Behaviors

Over our time as parent coaches, we've seen three tendencies parents have that get in the way of supporting their children with their feelings. They are often inherent traits or habits learned from family members and past experiences. Usually, these tendencies come from wanting to help, which we know all of you will relate to at some point in your parenting.

Sometimes, parents unintentionally (or purposefully) shut down their children's emotions or take on too much and become overwhelmed alongside their children; some tend to offer solutions too quickly. These are all common reactions, so let's go through each of them one by one, and you can note which ones you have a penchant for yourself.

Dismissal and Avoidance

Witnessing your child's intense emotions can be tough for any parent. It's tempting to downplay these feelings with reassurances, like "Don't be nervous, it's just a test," or to dismiss them as overreactions, such as "It's ridiculous to be upset over a celebrity breakup." You might find yourself exhausted by the constant emotional roller coaster, leading you to erupt, "You are overreacting!" or go completely quiet when you've had enough. If you grew up in a home where your feelings were often disregarded, it might be challenging for you to embrace your child's emotional expressions. You might find yourself uncomfortable with any displays of emotion, whether they're positive or negative.

The problem is that being critical or dismissive of children's moods in any way can make them feel uncomfortable, ashamed, or invisible—or all three. Dismissiveness threatens the connection between you because invariably, the child feels like their emotions don't count or like they're a disappointment to you. April shared in a group, "My parents always sent me to my room when I got upset as a kid. I was supposed to 'pull myself together,' but it never helped. I just sat there and thought about how embarrassed my parents were that I was upset. I couldn't help but cry, and it felt so awful."

Taking On Your Child's Feelings

Yolanda said, "When my daughter tells me that people at school call her a teacher's pet, I can't stand it. It reminds me of when I was bullied. I know she can tell."

Sometimes, it's so hard to see your child suffering that you feel the pain right alongside them. Some parents take on their child's overwhelm because it's a real struggle to know that you can't shield your children from the world. As Marta said, "When Valeria says she's anxious to leave me for school in case something bad happens, I can barely listen to her talk about it. The other day over breakfast, I told her abuela that it's tearing me apart to see her hurt like this."

It's natural to sympathize or empathize with your child when they're anxious. But when your worries are as big, if not bigger, than theirs, your needs take over. Your child won't have the space to figure out how they themselves feel about a situation, or become equipped to find a solution, because they will be pre-occupied with your emotions. They're left helpless, thinking, "Wait, I have the problem, but you are so upset you can't help me. What I'm worried about must be truly unsolvable, even for Mom." Watch out for moments when your own reactions are getting in the way of helping your child deal with theirs.

Teaching at the Wrong Time

If your child comes to you on the verge of tears before school, upset because they still don't know what to wear for Historical Fiction Day that morning, your first instinct might be to teach them a new technique for managing their time. However, when kids are overwhelmed by strong emotions, they're not in the right state of mind to learn. Calm them first. You can always teach them later.

This can be tricky because often the instinct is to give your child a solution you know can help in the moment. The rub with the tendency to teach at these times is that it will be counter-productive because the brain isn't fully functioning, making children unable to retain what you've shared. This means you will have to repeat yourself later, which is bound to cause frustration for everyone. In fact, offering a lesson in these moments of heightened emotion actually shuts down a child's receptivity to change. Parents tell us they want to say just the right thing so the lightbulb will go off in their child's head and they will remember the lesson forever. When a parent tries to teach a lesson during a heated interaction it ends in irritation and, often, tears.

Guidance must come in between tense moments, not during. Later in this chapter, we'll explain how to work with emotions and behaviors by making a Plan to Cope (PTC).

. . .

Now that you understand the tendencies that may hold you back, let's look at how to raise a child who can understand and talk about how they feel instead of holding in the hurt or resorting to negative behaviors.

Allow Feelings

When you make space for and allow your child's feelings, they also develop a vocabulary and understanding of what's going on inside them. These are essential building blocks for learning how to deal with hard feelings: first, they need to identify and acknowledge when they feel worried; then, you can help them find tools to manage it.

So first, let's examine ways you can help your child recognize and articulate their feelings.

Teach About Feelings

An easy way to explain feelings to your children is that the mind has a team of characters, each with a different feeling. One might feel happy, another might feel nervous, another might feel sad, and they work together like a squad to help you in different situations. Each of these pals has something important to tell you at different times: they help you figure out how you feel and what you need. Like if you're lonely, you might need some time with a classmate. Getting to know your emotions and talking about them helps the tough times get a bit easier.

Phoenix, age 9, described their moods as cities: "I'm very Seattle in winter right now. Dark and rainy. Nobody talk to me!" On happier days, they'd say they felt "very sunny Los Angeles." They had their meteorology down, and when they went to sleep-away camp, they continued to use this code in letters back home.

Welcome All Feelings with Curiosity

It's essential to create an environment where everyone talks about feelings, so your child knows theirs are welcome. Make space for all emotions, good and bad. Imagine your child's feelings as guests at the dinner table. Rather than shooing those pesky visitors away by saying, "Hey, you're cranky; perk up!" say, "Oh, feeling blue today, huh? Those days happen to me, too." Telling a child that their feelings are OK goes a long way to helping you stay connected emotionally and get the cooperation you are looking for.

Kids learn very quickly which feelings are acceptable to a parent and which are not. If you ask, "So, great day at school?" and you're uncomfortable hearing about a bad day, they'll keep their real emotions inside. Instead, show your child that the full spectrum of emotions is acceptable by asking them, "Let's hear your lemons and lollipops of the day," and maybe share yours first. This cues your children that you can handle the sour and sweet in life.

Here are other ways to help your child feel welcome to share their emotions. Saying these things will help you build trust with your child and motivate them to share their worries with you next time:

- Encourage them when they share a feeling: "I really appreciate the way you can talk to me about how you feel."

- Tell them you value talking about feelings: "It's always brave to say what's on your mind, and so important."

- Let them know you are available: "I'm always here to listen, so you don't have to be alone when things get tough."

- Support emotional expression: Instead of saying, "Don't cry," try "Crying is a good way to get the sad out."

There's plenty of time for you to educate children on how to handle disappointment or how to have gratitude, but in the exact moments they share their feelings, tell yourself, "I can calmly handle their emotions," and show them with words.

Remember, your child is learning to talk about and express their feelings by observing you. When you see that they're experiencing a feeling, name it out loud to help them understand what they're feeling. Mirror their emotions by saying, "It sounds like you were disappointed," or "I know you're scared." Suppose you suspect your child is anxious about your upcoming business trip. You might say, "Maybe you're feeling worried about me being away from home."

Start incorporating feelings as a topic of conversation when things are calm, like "Today I got so impatient waiting forty-five minutes for the doctor; I was thinking about how much I have to do and felt annoyed and desperate for them to call my name." For your bigger feelings, find places to vent to your friends and get support outside your child's view. Better to do that than using your kids as mini therapists.

Validate, Validate, Validate

Trust two child therapists: whatever upsets your child is a massive deal to them, no matter how minor it might seem to you. When you validate their concerns, even the paper cuts and dropped ice cream cones, you become that safe person with whom they can share everything. Validating a child's emotions makes them feel heard and supported, which can reduce their need to express feelings through negative behaviors.

When your child's friend is out sick or they aren't chosen to play four square, that is a significant event in their day, even if it sounds, well, childish. Show them you get what they're saying through every snot-nosed, irrational conversation. Understand that a day when baseball practice is canceled for rain is a total tragedy in their life because, at their age, baseball is what's most important to them. When your child complains about their sibling, say, "Being annoyed that your little sister wants to play with your friends is totally understandable."

In the same way, when your child is angry, say, "I can hear that you are angry; it's OK to be mad." When they are upset that you forgot to bring home the poster board they needed, try, "I completely understand why you're bummed about that." Tell them how common it is to feel bad when someone says hurtful things and that everyone feels frustrated when it's hard to comprehend something new.

By stepping into your kid's shoes, you join their team and help them feel less alone: "I know performing in front of people is scary." If it's relevant you can add, "When I was your age, I felt the same way when I had gymnastics meets." You have the power to make your child feel comfortable with having emotions rather than like a disappointment for sharing their feelings with you.

Displacement on Display

Sometimes, your child might react to one thing when they're actually worried about something else. This is called displacement. Imagine that your child worked all weekend putting the finishing touches on their project, and then they tell you they got a whole grade lower than they expected. After school, anything you say or do doesn't seem to be right—they're irritable about everything but insist "Nothing is wrong!" You might intuit that they are upset about what happened in class and feel safer showing those angry feelings to you instead of the teacher. You could be right, as this is common for kids.

Use detective-like skills to get underneath what is happening by looking for clues that your child might be having emotions about something else. Here are a few situations where you might see this in action:

- Telling you that you're the meanest mom when a friend snubbed them that day in school

* Crying over PB&J when it's their favorite snack—after they lost screen privileges

* Zeroing in on forgetting their water bottle when they have a big swim meet coming up

* Refusing to go to sports or activities when they found out their closest grandparent was sick

Your child's understanding of their emotions is still under construction, so they can only sometimes identify the origin of their feelings. Often, we see the emotions coming out sideways at you rather than at their best friend, school, or whatever is truly bothering them inside. Even if you figure out what's really going on, rather than call out why they are upset, simply validate what they're telling you. That's what they need in that moment.

Help Worry Make Sense

If you have a child with a fear (or many), explain what's happening so they can understand it better. Don't shy away from using words like "worry" or "anxiety"—they aren't going to make anything worse. Kids like having information and tools to feel more in control.

Here's a script you can use. Adapt it as necessary to meet your children's needs. Say, "Worry is something everyone feels. Sometimes, when you're anxious about something, the worried voice in your brain gets loud, trying to warn you that something bad might happen. That part of your brain is useful if a bear is chasing you because it helps you escape the bear! It says, 'Run!'

Or if you're trying to cross the street, that voice tells you to look out for fast cars. But sometimes, the voice in your brain is working too hard; it might be making you feel like something bad will happen even though you are cozy in bed. I'll teach you ways to help quiet the nervous voice so you can feel more relaxed. We will practice these tools so that you will know what to do when worry comes!"

Teach your child to talk about their worry voice from a distance in a fun, sometimes even silly way. Some kids call worry "sticky thoughts" or name it. Kaden, age 11, named the rational and decision-making part of his brain "Albert Einstein" and the worried part "Nervous Ned." Teach them to tell "Ned" when he gets over-worried that everything is OK and that they can use the helpful tools to get "Albert" back in charge. Have your child make up their own names.

Remember that children have a thriving imagination. Use that to calm them! Alexis, age 8, had an imaginary newt that she'd talk about when she felt nervous. The newt reminded her of a funny scene in the movie *Matilda*, making the situation feel less scary. She would press her hands together as if holding the reptile and whisper to her mom, "The newt is back. He's scared because it's almost time for my recital." This was their unique way of giving shape and dimension to her worry.

It also brings some lightness to the moment. That's what Mason, age 10, did when he dubbed his fear about bedtime "Worry the Wonder Farters." Tizita, age 12, when nervous and excited about something new, calls it "nervouscited." Have your child come up with something creative to personify their anxieties. It gets them on board with working on emotional regulation.

Teaching Your Child to Listen to Their Body

You want your children to understand how their feelings can affect them physically. This helps them recognize and handle uncomfortable emotions more effectively. Help them see that their body communicates through signals. If their heart starts racing, it's not just by chance but a sign of nervousness. Sweaty palms might mean they're worried about something, not just hot. Getting tired at Grandpa's assisted living facility could mean they're overwhelmed. By noticing these vital physical connections, your kids start to identify and manage their feelings better.

· Following Clues to Feelings

Put on your sleuthing hat to figure out when your child has feelings they don't yet know how to communicate constructively. Children are unlikely to say, "I grind my teeth when I'm frustrated," without you helping them make these connections.

Let's look at what these caregivers have figured out:

- Andre's small 6-year-old body sat slumped on the couch, shoulders forward with his face buried in Book 6 of his most recent sci-fi series. Since his parents got divorced, they noticed that he wasn't asking for playdates anymore. They realized they most often see a book cover rather than his actual face and learned that when Andre is sad, he isolates himself from his friends.

- When it came time to go on a sleepover, Sydney, age 8, would tell her mom, "I have a stomachache," even though she had excitedly packed her overnight bag and picked out the pj's she would wear days before. Now Mom realizes that when Sydney mentions having a stomachache during transition periods, it can indicate that she is worried.

- Nora, age 12, and in full preteen years, took a cooler approach by icing Dad out when she was upset with him. She'd saunter right through the living room, headphones on, saying nothing as she passed by him. She didn't even look in his direction. Nora doesn't use words to indicate that she's upset—her dad knows it by her frosty attitude that she is angry and needs time to "cool off."

- When José is scared or overwhelmed, his 10-year-old face begins to look glazed over, and his body becomes very still. It's almost like his personality leaves the room but his body is still there. His moms try to talk to him and say, "Hey, what's wrong? You are not even listening!" but his expression doesn't change. José's parents learned that this "frozen" state means that he is too overwhelmed at the moment to communicate.

· *Help Them Make Connections*

Help your child connect their emotions to their behaviors. It's a skill they'll develop the more they do it. First, explain to your child why it's important to understand what's going on inside them. Say, "The more we know about how our body sends us signals, the better. Because when we know we're worried or upset, we can do something to help those feelings go down."

Tell them, "Some people's bellies rumble when they're nervous, their hearts race when they feel excited, and tears well up in their eyes when they're sad. The body tells us important information!" Ask them, "How do you think bodies talk?" Use yourself as an example. In a calm moment, mention to them: "When I'm stressed, I tap my foot a lot. Dad starts pacing when he's got an important meeting coming up. Have you ever noticed that?" Kids need to know what they feel in their body to change their behavior.

You can ask, "Does your body get tight, hot, cold, antsy?" There's no right or wrong answer; you are just helping them recognize their body's signals. Ask periodically, and if they don't detect much or anything at all, week after week, tell them, "It's OK if it takes a while to notice a body sensation."

Then, help them connect their feelings and their behaviors, and be sure to speak lovingly and empathetically about it as you do: "It seems you get frustrated when you have to read out loud at home because you don't like to mess up. It makes you want to shut the book and shove it under the couch, and sometimes you do!" Ask them, "Hey, have you ever noticed that it's hard to fall asleep before you have a big game, and you get up for water way more times? That might be because of your worry about the tournament."

Be gentle and include yourself, too, as a way of normalizing their experience. "I notice you scrunch your face when you're watching a scary movie! I wonder if it's because you're a little bit afraid. When I get scared, I pick at my nails and sometimes I speak really quickly." When you communicate this way, it helps lower any shame kids might feel about their behaviors and gives them a compassionate perspective of what's going on.

Naming connections can kick up feelings of embarrassment. For children who don't like it when you point out their behaviors, throw out casual statements about yourself here and there: "I don't like jump scares, so I'm always clutching a couch pillow!" The goal is, over time, for your child to be able to identify their patterns and speak about them.

A child who can say, "Sometimes, when I have to turn off my video game, I get so mad I want to throw a shoe at the wall," is a child who is on his way to taking deep breaths instead of staining your wall with his muddy Nikes.

· *Use a Body Map*
Help your child create a visual representation of their body, which will assist them in better identifying their cornucopia of feelings, including worry. As we said, understanding emotions and body sensations takes practice. Have fun with this!

First, have your child draw the outline of a gingerbread body on a piece of paper. You could even use butcher paper to make a life-size version. Choose one emotion and ask, "Can you draw what your body feels like in different places when you get worried? Does your tummy hurt? Can you draw that? What color do you want to make your throat when it feels tight and dry?" On another day, choose a new emotion: anger, joy, jealousy, boredom, and so forth.

They can use colors, shapes, lines, and textures to show how they experience emotions. Dylan, age 7, used a blue marker and colored over his head and shoulders when he felt sad, and made thick orange spirals in his fists to show what anger looks like.

Whatever you do, do not correct the details in the picture.

Allow your child to draw purple knives around the belly or red lava coming out of their ears, whatever it may be. Trust us, it's a fun and effective way to build an understanding of how emotions and physical sensations are closely intertwined.

Guide Behaviors

In this section, we'll examine practical coping strategies for your child to manage intense emotions. The key is to "teach ahead" by introducing these skills during calm moments—well before stressful situations arise. This way, your child can practice and become familiar with the tools, making them ready to use when needed.

Repetition and reminders will make a difference as your child learns these new skills. Think of it like building any other habit—it takes time and consistent practice. Avoid teaching these techniques during tense or emotional times; they're only effective when everyone is relaxed and receptive.

Here's a simple way to explain these exercises to your child: "We all have big feelings sometimes, and we need tools to help manage them. Just like we brush our teeth every day, we'll practice using these coping skills regularly. We'll find the ones that work best for us, just like picking your favorite school supplies for class. And remember, everyone—even Mom, Grandpa, and your stepsister—needs ways to handle their emotions."

Name It and Scale It

Teach your kids to manage emotions by naming what they feel. Explain that worry likes to hide in the dark and fester and that sharing it out loud with you or a trusted friend or sibling will help them feel better. It even works when they say it in their heads (e.g., *I am so anxious about what my teacher thinks of me*). Naming the feeling can help lower their anxiety, even if they don't say it out loud.

Introduce a "worry thermometer" to help kids visualize and rate their emotions. They can create a thermometer with levels from 1 (minor worry) to 10 (major worry). For instance, ask them to rate giving a speech at school or being in a tall building.

When problems arise, encourage them to categorize their concerns by marking them on the thermometer. Dominic, age 6, marked police sirens as an 8, but during dinner with his mom, he identified his worry level as a 3, noting the absence of an actual siren outside. Briana, age 9, notices a drop from her usual 7 to a 4 when she plays catch with her dad.

This activity teaches children that their emotional intensity can fluctuate depending on context and that they have the power to bring it down with a coping tool, which fosters a sense of mastery over their feelings. You won't believe how effective this technique can be for kids learning to recognize that emotions ebb and flow, and that even the toughest feelings dissipate with time.

Take a Breath

Kids don't necessarily love to be told to breathe deeply. It's become every exasperated gym teacher's go-to method to bring an unruly group to order. But you can remind your kids that a few conscious breaths instantly increase their ability to focus, which is helpful in ballet, debate, and laser tag. It might help to mention celebrities like Michael Jordan and Katy Perry talk about how much breathing and self-calming exercises help them do what they do so very well. Google your kids' heroes to find out if they're meditators. A lot of super-well-known people are.

Get in the habit of taking three deep breaths with your child before bed. Have them put a hand on their tummy and feel the breath fill it up "like a belly balloon." Trace their hand with each breath: up a finger, breathe in, and down a finger, breathe out, and repeat. Encourage children to sing their hearts out in the car—it's a great way to see how breathing deeply, especially from the diaphragm, Broadway-style, makes us feel a little better. Don't correct them, and don't be afraid to start small. Even one intentional deep breath a day can feel like a relief.

Move Around

Encourage your child to engage in physical activity to help process pent-up emotions. Outdoor activities like bike riding or rock climbing can be particularly effective. Alternatively, a spirited dance session in the living room can be a great way to dispel frustration. For kids who enjoy a challenge, pull out your stopwatch and set up a playful relay race that includes five jumping jacks and some balance poses.

Let your child discover activities that soothe them when they're stressed and offer a variety of suggestions beforehand to help them find their preferred outlet. Explain to them, "Sometimes, when you're feeling crummy, moving and getting your heart rate up is a good way to get that stress through your system." Then, see if they can name five movement activities they can do in those moments. Try them out while they're calm and explain simply, "Today we're going to try number one on your list for when you get angry: 'Jump rope for five minutes!'"

If you notice they seem calmer after doing something active, say, "Scootering around the block really helped chill us out. I feel less stressed about my to-do list. What about you? Do you feel different?" Brainstorm with them when it might be a good time to get outside, like before a stressful day.

Tap Into the Five Senses

We've mentioned how important it is for parents to tap into their senses to find calm. Kids should do it, too. The best way we know is to share the idea as a really cool trick (or, better yet, a secret superpower) they can use anytime, anywhere, and without anyone knowing they are doing it. Say, "Guess what? When you focus on any one of your five senses, it helps you quiet down the worry voice."

Tell your child to choose one of their senses to focus on. For example, ask them to look around and name out loud the things they see: "Can you find three objects that catch your eye right now and describe them to me?" For younger children, ask them to spot all things of the same color. Your child may like to listen to five sounds or feel five textures in the immediate area.

Teach them to sip a warm or cold drink slowly, or bite into something, noticing textures and tastes. Your child may like listening to a recording of a cozy wood fire crackling or the soothing patter of rain on a rooftop, taking a bubble bath, or stroking the fur of a family pet (or a stuffed animal). Like everything else, explore broadly and let them decide which sensations help them settle down in the moment. Practice often. In a quiet moment, help them make the connection by telling them what you notice: "When you were lying in the grass just now, you seemed so relaxed!"

Prioritize the Outdoors

Embrace nature for its mental health benefits to the entire family; it has a tremendous impact. Children need to have unstructured time to sweat and play. Assess how much of their day they spend outdoors; if it's not much, make a change. Prioritize nature when planning summers or weekends. Encourage outdoor gatherings with friends; opt for a picnic on the grass over a movie indoors. Plan a camping trip where they can hear the distant hoot of an owl or see the enchanting sight of fireflies.

Let them be in awe of a valley view, feel wet sand between their toes, or experience the thrill of bodysurfing on the waves. Activities like flying a kite, throwing a Frisbee, or taking a pre-bedtime walk are beneficial for reducing anxiety. Nature cultivates mindfulness, drawing attention to the intricate dance of leaves, the songs of birds, and the earthy touch of dirt. Whether your child is gazing at the stars or studying tree bark, nature grounds them in the present, breaking the cycle of anxious thoughts.

Set Up a Chill Zone

Designate a space in the house to hide out if they need a break. It could be their bedroom or a cozy corner with a beanbag chair. Play up the no-worries vibe with glow-in-the-dark stars or a lava lamp. Anything that's relaxing works. Old blankets, slippers, and comfy clothes set a tone that says, "Ahhh." Jada said, "My mama Jenny gave me one of her old sweatshirts to wear when I feel upset—it's so soft and even has holes in it from when she wore it; I love to snuggle up in it." Sit in the chill zone with your child and ask them, "How can we make it even cozier here for when you're having a crummy day?"

Self-Express Through Art and Music

Kids love to unload their thoughts through writing and benefit from the freedom of having something nobody else will examine or judge. Please don't, under any circumstances, read it. If your child finds out—which they usually do—they will experience it as a huge breach of trust. Some children might enjoy writing in a designated parent-child journal, because sometimes it's easier to say something in writing than out loud. If you are lucky enough to have a child willing to do this, be sure to write back only validating and supportive statements, like "I understand why you feel that way," or "That day was hard! Thank you for sharing with me," or "I love you." Keep this an advice-free space.

If a journal's not their thing, encourage them to compose a song, make a comic strip about the family pet, or construct a "graffiti wall" on panels of taped-up poster board. This can be especially valuable for children who struggle to articulate their feelings in words. Again, don't direct them what to draw, and never correct or critique what they've made—just provide the supplies and applaud their hard work. Their drawing may seem related or unrelated to their worries, but they are still processing feelings. Get them a canvas and pens and watch them go!

Some kids really enjoy making "mood playlists" with songs to match what they're feeling. Karim, age 12, says, "I have my 'Sad Boy' playlist for when things go wrong at school. I go to my room, put on my headphones, and listen. My favorite artists just get me, and it helps me feel better." Another preteen we know plays her "Happy Sunrise Beats" to lift everyone's spirits in the morning and her "Pregame Anxiety Medicine" playlist to calm her nerves before every chess tournament. Listening to music helps kids feel connected and understood, reminding them that they're not alone in their feelings.

Teach Affirming Phrases

Lend your pearls of wisdom for tough moments. Encourage your child to say to themselves, "Things are easier the second time around," or "I can do it," during moments of worry or before a big event. Teach them to recite, "It only feels this way *for now*, but I know even the worst feelings will pass," or "Just because I'm imagining something bad, it doesn't mean it's going to happen!" If your kids welcome it, put these callouts on Post-its on a mirror or in their backpack.

Role-Play

Practice what your child might say or do in various situations when they tend to get worried. If they are nervous to order a drink at a coffee shop, pretend to be a barista in the kitchen and have them try it out with you. If they fear presenting in class, act out a faux school presentation at the dinner table and be sure to build in several deep breaths. Coming up with scripts together and playing out scenarios for any complicated situation goes a long way in building confidence.

Create a Calm Box

Help your child put together a shoebox full of activities that bring their attention to the present moment and relax the nervous system. Remind them that anything that requires quiet, undisturbed focus can help rest their brain and improve their mood when they're feeling off. Let your child choose what goes inside—it should be personal.

They can add plain paper and markers, coloring or paint-by-numbers books, Legos, fidgets, slime, a book, brainteasers, or a deck of cards. Some kids will claim that their video game or scrolling through social media or videos calms them down. But we have a clear "no" stance when it comes to screens as a vehicle for calm in these moments—neither for them nor you.

Once you have your calm box set up, you can guide your child to it when a difficult feeling arises: "I know you're feeling worried. How about we look at your calm box and see if there's something in there you can focus on for a minute?" Practice using the box during times of calm—even five minutes a day—to help children recognize it as a tool to use when they feel upset.

Make a "Worry Holder"

Create a place where anxieties can be temporarily set aside. Encourage your child to jot down their fears on a piece of paper and place it in a designated envelope or pouch, symbolically removing the worry from their mind. If they like, they can personalize this worry holder with decorations. Whenever they feel overwhelmed, you can say, "Write down what you are scared about and place it in the pouch!" This can be especially helpful at night, assisting them in letting go of troubling thoughts before sleep.

Schedule a "Worry Window"

If your kid has free-floating anxiety or feels overpowered by emotions that pop up only to derail them, try this: schedule a fifteen-minute window later in the day for them to worry. You can say, "I know you're feeling worried. I have an idea that might help. When you get home, I'll set a timer and you can think all about it, scream into your pillow, or talk it out with me until the timer goes off." Believe it or not, they might not even remember to do this when they get home.

Practice Together

As a family, try one of these tools daily for a week. Endeavor to be consistent. You will be a much better teacher if you go into this knowing the process can get bumpy. Even if they reject your suggestions now, children will remember them and are likely to start using these calming tools as they get older. You're sowing the seeds for self-regulation.

As always, be patient. Real change takes time!

What to Say in the Moment: Allow Feelings to Guide Behaviors

Now that you've equipped your child with various coping skills, you can guide their behavior using these tools when needed. Children often express big emotions through behavior or harsh words. Remember, you can maintain boundaries while still being supportive.

Here's how it might sound: "I hear you're upset about having to leave the house and stop painting. It's OK to feel annoyed. We need to get your brother to practice; grab your favorite fidget spinner and get in the car. Let's chat about how you feel after we drop him off."

Check out the chart on the next page for more examples of how to allow your child's feelings while holding limits and guiding them to something more constructive.

YOUR CHILD'S FEELING	YOUR CHILD'S BEHAVIOR	ALLOW FEELINGS TO GUIDE BEHAVIORS
Anger	Throwing something	"It's totally understandable to be mad that practice got canceled. Tossing my phone across the room is not allowed. We can go outside and shoot some anger hoops together, or you can shoot alone. Which would you like?"
Overwhelm	Refusing an activity	"I know you feel overwhelmed just having moved to this apartment. All your feelings are welcome; skipping meals is not an option. Come join us for a short dinner. What feels helpful, splashing your face with cold water or taking three deep breaths to reset? A dinner break will help you feel more relaxed."
Worry	Stalling at bedtime	"I understand you're nervous about the spelling bee and want to keep practicing, but you need your rest. Go brush your teeth and get in bed. Would you like me to scratch your back to help you relax?"

Use positive feedback to reinforce the behavior, build confidence, and help them connect how using this tool helped ease their anxieties: "Great job, I noticed you grabbed the Rubik's Cube when you got annoyed by your brother's loud chewing. That's a really good way to handle a challenge."

Your child might try on ideas and take your suggestions. Other times, guiding them to a positive coping skill will take a lot of repetition and practice.

Every parent has power struggles with their kids. They might talk back, you get annoyed, and voices get heightened. They could feel super anxious and act out when you need to make them go somewhere. Siblings may get involved, and feelings get hurt. Or they exclaim, "You don't get me at all!" It can be challenging—and seemingly impossible sometimes—to stay loving and warm in these moments.

Let's talk about what to do when there's an inevitable explosion of feelings and you wish it had gone differently.

What to Say Later: Repair What Happened and Plan for Next Time

After a tense moment, children tend to feel embarrassed of themselves or concerned that you will be upset with them for a long time. A simple, straightforward conversation is necessary after everyone has calmed down and cooled off. Expect to have lots of these dialogues as your child is growing up because things go south fairly often!

When you take the lead in repairing feelings after difficult interactions, you help you and your child stay emotionally connected. After this conversation, you can establish clear and consistent limits for future moments and review helpful choices they can make.

Use the following steps to recover from what happened and make a plan for next time. You will notice that the conversation involves a lot of empathy up front and some creative troubleshooting at the end.

Step 1: *Review What Happened and Empathize with Your Child*

First, use your Set the Tone and validation skills to express understanding without shaming them about what happened. For example, you might say, "Earlier today, you had a hard time with your brother because he took your seat. You ended up punching him in the arm. I know you really wanted to sit next to me, and that move came right out of you."

Or maybe there was a tense moment between the two of you: "When we were talking before school, we said some harsh words. You said I'm the worst mom, and that tells me you must have been having a really hard time because you only say things like that when you're really upset. I can tell you didn't feel like I was listening."

End with "I want us to figure out a way to do this differently next time."

Step 2: *Repair Your Side*

This is about owning your mistakes first to show that you are taking responsibility for your behavior. If you turn to their missteps first, they may feel flustered, and kids who feel ashamed are not very good listeners. Kids don't know how to apologize or take responsibility for their actions unless you demonstrate how. If you mess up, find a way to make it right in the same way you'd want them to apologize to you and others. Instead of forcing an apology from them, let them learn from your example.

What this means is that if you lose your temper, don't ignore it, don't pretend it never happened, don't give them the silent treatment, and don't justify it. Instead, demonstrate that you can take accountability and be a "work in progress." So, grab hold of your Set the Tone skills and explain simply: "I yelled, and no matter what, I shouldn't have raised my voice at you like that." Refrain from adding why you did what you did. This is not an exercise in explaining yourself but in owning what you could have done better and what you will try to do in the future. Leave the word "but" out of your apology.

Here's another example:

"I am sorry I yelled at you, but I am so frustrated with your behavior."

Try this instead:

"I got angry at you yesterday when we were on our way to karate practice. I know my voice got way too loud, and I'm sorry I got so mad. Next time, I'll take a breath and wait to talk so I don't yell when I'm feeling that way."

Ask, "What was it like for you when I yelled? I wonder if it ever feels too loud or scary for you when I'm upset." And don't be afraid to hear them say, "Yes, it feels awful." You can say, "Yeah, it feels too loud when I yell. I get it. I need to work on it." Or you can respond to what they say with "Thank you for sharing your feelings with me. I am glad you are being open with me."

Eventually, as they grow older, they will emulate your behavior. Lead by example, and they will soak it in. A repair might end in a big hug or an "I love you." If kids tell you they're sorry, keep it simple and say, "I appreciate that. I'm sorry, too." If they need time or space after this part and aren't ready to keep talking, know that is normal. If so, give them some space and finish the steps below later. If they seem unsettled or frazzled, it's OK to take a break for some hours or days—just be sure to come back to the conversation at another time.

Step 3: *Set Limits and Impart Family Values*

Next is your opportunity to set limits and review what needs to happen next time. Don't create rules on the fly, change them randomly, or punish them out of the blue. The ol' "That's it, you're grounded!" or "Off your screens for speaking to me that way!" moments make them anxious. Instead, after emotions have settled, take the time to review and clarify expectations with your child, making any necessary adjustments to ensure everyone is set up for success.

Share how things will be different going forward and lean on family values. Use a firm but loving voice. Melanie, Dasha's step-mom, says, "I know you're struggling to pick your outfit before school each day and it makes us late. This morning, I raised my voice and I'm sorry. I get that it takes time to pick out an outfit you like; doing so can't make us late. Being on time is important in our family, and it communicates to the people we are going to meet that they matter to us. Going forward, I'm going to have you pick your outfit the night before instead."

Family values help children learn to respect and care for each other and steer behaviors and actions. If your child takes your favorite necklace and you find it tangled on her doll, explain what it means to respect other people's property. Pick one topic at a time in these dialogues and teach your children about everything from kindness and gratitude to screen time and house rules.

Carlos shared that sleep is essential in their family, and he set a limit with a clearly defined consequence: "I know you didn't want to stop your game last night. Keep in mind that sleep needs to happen, and it's my job to keep you healthy. Going forward, if you don't turn it off at eight fifteen p.m. and plug it in in the hallway, there will be no screen time the following day. None. I want you to know in advance so that you know what to expect."

Be fair and age-appropriate with your limits and allow kids to reset and try again the following day. And don't waver: if your children are *sometimes* allowed to eat dinner in front of the TV when they beg but other times not, they will not learn to understand or follow limits. Loving and consistent boundaries give your children the structure they need, and that consistency helps them succeed more each time.

Step 4: *Make a Plan to Cope (PTC)*

Lastly, make a PTC for what they will do to manage their feelings differently next time. When you encounter resistance ("I'm not going to Aunt Erin's house again for dinner!") or back talk ("Why should I listen to you?"), it's usually a sign that they need more help managing their emotions.

Try something like this: "Being angry is totally OK but ignoring me is not. I want us to have a plan for what you and I can try in these moments. What do you think you can do instead?"

Often, they might say, "I don't know." Give them suggestions from the coping tools you taught them and brainstorm new ideas together. Ask them, "Do you want to take a few minutes in your chill zone when you get irritated?" or "If you feel mad at your sister at dinner, would you like to have your trading cards on the table to sort for a few minutes?"

You can state, "There is no hitting or screaming, and I want to help you find something else to try." Commit to your end of the deal: "I'll work on my tone and take a break if I start to feel frustrated, pause, and use a coping tool." Set the stage for their future growth and progress. They may not take you up on it this time, but they will hear you and try it eventually.

Make a plan for managing anxiety, like this: "When your worries show up after school, you can cozy up with music and your favorite stuffed animal and draw in your journal for twenty minutes to unwind. Let's try this today after school and see how you feel."

Practice tools as a family. Come up with a code word, like "bananas," "salamander," or "tuba," which mean you all need to take a five-minute breather. Hearing the word is intended to make you laugh and break the tension. If you use a code word, honor the plan to pause regardless of who says it and why.

Put your heads together to develop a creative plan everyone can handle. It takes trial and error. For example, the Williams family played a particular song when screen time ended to reduce arguments in the house. It took a while to get into the groove (it always does), but eventually, the change worked. No one said, "Thanks, Dad, for figuring out an easier way to make us turn off our favorite TV show," but the song still helped to cue the kids to get ready for bed without a fight every night.

Isabella's family of four ran on high energy and often had difficulty communicating calmly, especially in the mornings and at bedtime. After a few months of SAFER Parenting, she told us, "The big emotions in our house aren't gone by any stretch, but I can see the light at the end of the tunnel. Every encounter used to end in someone crying, but we're now better able, in our ways, to take a break and try a tool. Some of us struggle to realize we need to settle ourselves down," she said as she winked at her husband. "But the kids—really all of us—are beginning to catch moments of calm, even sometimes talking through things that would have ended in frustration."

Above all, give children room to learn and get things wrong, be flexible, and collaborate with them. Don't expect a PTC to work the first time—think "progress, not perfection." But do it often, so discussing a plan with your children is as usual as checking on the weather. You may think, "I've tried to talk to my kid, and she just rejects the conversation and tells me to go away." Don't give up. Keep having an open dialogue and set up PTCs. You'll get there with super-consistent practice, we promise.

• • •

Understanding and managing feelings is critical, and the tools in this chapter play an essential role in helping your children develop strong emotional awareness and build a toolbox to cope with worry. You have learned that children's ability to put their feelings into words starts at home.

As children grow, help them strengthen their emotional vocabulary and coping abilities, practice with them, and hold limits consistently. Apologize to them when you inevitably lose your cool. Every time you do something new, it's a win in our book.

Questions and Reflections for Deeper Thinking

Once again, let's take this discussion a step further. With the prompts below, we encourage you to jot down your thoughts and feelings openly. Explore how the ideas we've discussed resonate with your daily parenting experiences—from morning squabbles at the breakfast table to bedtime routines. We're here to support you as you make these connections and discover new approaches to everyday parenting challenges.

• Were you allowed to freely express your emotions as a child, or were certain feelings considered off-limits? How were you disciplined, and did you have coping tools to use when "big feelings" came up?

• Reflect on what helps calm your child. How can the tips from this chapter help them handle anxiety, especially in new or challenging situations?

• Which of your child's emotions are you most comfortable handling and which do you tend to ignore or dread?

• Did anyone apologize to you as a child? How often do you apologize now for losing your temper?

• In what ways have you been inconsistent with rules at home? What clearer boundaries could you set that still allow your child to express feelings?

Five

Form Identity

Every parent hopes for their child to grow up to have strong self-esteem. As children experience the people and places around them, they start to build an identity—they learn words for race, ethnicity, and gender, and they start to gain a vocabulary to describe who they are: "I'm smart and I'm a strong swimmer, but I'm really bad at drawing." As they figure themselves out, it's important that they take pride in their identity, interests, and personality traits. It's disheartening to hear your child criticize a part of themselves, perhaps it even feels familiar to the voice in your own head. As their parent, you get to help your child form a solid inner core that leads to higher self-worth and lower anxiety levels.

The relationship you have with your child and how you talk about them on a day-to-day basis matters. When children receive your acknowledgment of their accomplishments and capabilities, it strengthens their belief in themselves. You and the community around them have a major impact on how they see themselves and getting that approving support and sense of belonging counteracts self-doubt and feelings of inadequacy.

We were talking about the importance of confidence-building

in one of our parenting groups when Ani spoke up. "We've been trying really hard to help our son build his identity over the last few months, so we asked him one night at dinner to tell us who he is. He suggested we record him and share it with the group." Everyone was excited because, like a lot of kids, he loves a camera.

Vartan is 12 years old, tall for his age, and super slim, with dark brown, shaggy hair.

In his hoodie and backward baseball hat, he looked at the camera shyly and said, "I'm Vartan. I'm from Brooklyn—go Nets! I'm Armenian, and my cousins actually live in Armenia. I play goalie for my soccer team. I'm in the school play because I love to act, but Mom makes me play the trumpet, which I don't love." He sticks his tongue out to show disgust.

You could hear Mom laughing in the background and softly asking, "What else?"

Without missing a beat, he continued, "My favorite foods are lavash and pizza, but I don't like dolma. I love McDonald's, but Mom only lets us go there on special occasions." He looked at his mom and added sarcastically, "Which is, like, never . . . I love BTS, but System of a Down is my favorite Armenian band. It's Dad's favorite, too. I'm obsessed with FIFA, and I beat my dad at it in the last two games."

Vartan's mom was beaming because when they first came to the group, he was struggling with low self-esteem. Now, she saw big progress in the way he felt about himself after some new self-confidence tools (which we're about to share with you). Having a strong sense of self will serve as a metaphorical shield for your children that buffers them against worrying.

A Strong Identity Serves a Child for a Lifetime

As children grow, they discover so many new things about themselves. This period can be exciting and anxiety-inducing as kids begin to understand how they fit in with their family, their peers, and the world. Let's examine further how this strong identity aids your child.

They're Less Susceptible to Peer Pressure

Children need a solid foundation to navigate the wobbly years of adolescence, particularly now in a world flooded with fake advertisements, unrealistic beauty standards, and social media pressures. Otherwise, they may become overly dependent on the approval of others and vulnerable to peer pressure. Feeling good about who they are allows them to rely less on what others think and allows them to accept—and take pride in—being different.

Children who know their identity are less likely to get stuck when making choices. They are more decisive because they know what they want and can make judgments that reflect their goals and values. Build this layer of protection, and you will significantly reduce your child's reaction to anxiety-provoking outside coercion. So, when your daughter's friend says, "This is the only lip gloss you can wear," she can say, "Glad you like it! I love mine, too." And when the stakes get higher, they can make safe decisions about things that matter.

They Exude Greater Confidence

Feeling self-assured allows children to have less fear and go for what they want more readily. It enables them to take risks in approaching a new friend, taking on a new sport, or asking for a solo in the town theater summer musical. A child needs to believe they can try new, different, and possibly challenging things and set aspirational goals. Feeling strong in their identity builds optimism and a "can-do" attitude.

They Show Self-Compassion

Children with a strong sense of identity can find kinder, less harsh words for themselves when things get tough. For instance, instead of saying, "I'm not a good reader," a child can draw from the context of their identity and say, "I know I have to work harder at reading, but I also just moved to this country a few years ago, so I'm cutting myself some slack." Self-compassion helps to lift the burden of perfectionism and is a powerful antidote to anxiety.

They Recover Faster from Setbacks

Rather than criticize themselves or give up, children can clearly see a situation and identify all the factors that went into the outcome: "I forgot my homework because I didn't put the folder back into my backpack before bedtime. I should try doing that next time." Having this sense of self makes them feel confident to try again.

On the other hand, kids who don't see themselves in a good light tend to blame themselves and assume things won't change: "I forgot my homework because I'm a stupid person." We want kids who think, "I like who I am, and I can try again. I might still need to improve, but it doesn't mean I'm a bad person if I make a mistake."

They Have Healthier Relationships

Children with positive self-perception build healthier relationships. When they know themselves well, they are more likely to seek support and use coping strategies that lead to better stress management over time.

Children with solid self-esteem are also less likely to fall into "people-pleasing" tendencies with peers and adults because they understand their needs and limits. They're better at recognizing when something is not right for them at the moment or when they're too stretched, avoiding situations where they might agree just because they feel sorry for someone else. When children feel comfortable with themselves, they can kindly say they'd love to help but just can't right now. Their confidence helps them stick to their choices, rather than being swayed just because they feel bad for someone.

Above all, higher self-esteem directly correlates with better mental health. Kids with low self-esteem experience more mental health challenges like anxiety, depression, and eating disorders. Children need this positive sense of self within them to ward off ideas from others that they don't fit in, their body isn't perfect, or any other negative or pressurized message.

Your Attention Shapes Their Self-Image

Whether you know it or not, you are the person who has the most significant impact on what your child thinks about themselves. A child who believes they are valued by a parent will take that belief with them into the world and throughout adulthood. They will expect to be treated well by others and, in turn, identify and sidestep situations and relationships that don't treat them with the respect they deserve. Conversely, if a child picks up from you that they are a disappointment, they will grow into an adult who feels they are not well liked or are even a burden to others.

Chloe, age 10, says, "My dad is silly; he always tells me and my brother, 'You're my favorite humans on earth.' I shrug it off, but mostly, I love hearing it." In the same way, your child must know, "My parent loves me, even when we disagree; and even though we had a hard morning, they'll still be there for me tonight no matter what."

Children also need to know that you would go to great lengths to protect them. This is crucial for their sense of safety in the world. Zan, age 9, told us, "Mom would beat down walls to get to me if there was an earthquake. Dad once showed me that huge, green comic book character, The Hulk, and I could see Mom coming down the street to get me looking just like him," they said laughingly. As funny as it is to visualize Mom as The Hulk, Zan gave a great example of *knowing* Mom has their back.

As your kids start noticing themselves and others, you also want them to have a positive narrative about their personality, body, preferences, and abilities—all the beautiful and powerful parts of themselves. You have the opportunity to instill a positive way for them to think about themselves. The more children are celebrated by you and their community, the more they believe, "I am important, and I matter."

Community and Belonging Are Key

Supportive communities also play a big role in shaping your child's identity and sense of safety in the world. Belonging makes children feel part of something bigger and brings about more stability and inner peace. Having a place where they fit in helps combat feelings of being different from others, which can be very distressing for kids.

Out in the world, children hear tons of disapproving views about their culture, race, appearance, gender, and sexuality. They may pick up a harmful message at school that specific skin colors, body types, or family structures are better or worse than others.

For 8-year-old Bunma, it started with her lunch box. She loved rice and moo yong, a dish with shredded dried pork, but the other kids said the finely textured meat looked like "carpet hair." She cried when they made fun of her. Her mom, through her own tears, told the parenting group, "It's such a powerless feeling watching your child get tormented like that."

Bunma was a transracial adoptee, and it was important for her family to help her connect with her heritage. An elderly neighbor whom Bunma affectionately called Pah—a term used in Thai culture for someone older than your mom—became an inspiring figure in her life. After a tough day at school, Bunma and Pah bonded over their love for rice and moo yong. Pah could tell that Bunma felt embarrassed, and she explained that the dish's appearance, which most people don't know how to appreciate, is one more thing that makes Bunma's culture unique and special. Over the next few weeks, they spent more time getting comfortable in the Asian market, experimenting with different recipes for rice and moo yong, including teaching Bunma's mom how to make Pah's recipe for it.

These cooking sessions boosted Bunma's confidence and helped her embrace her culture of origin. Months later, she told her mom how the negative comments from classmates didn't bother her as much anymore. "I hate it when they are mean, not just to me but to anyone. And they don't know what they're missing. To them, it looks like the grossest thing ever, but it tastes like love to me. We know how yummy it tastes." The experience reinforced the sense of community and belonging that her parents and Pah were mirroring around her.

Roadblocks to Forming Identity

By now, you've seen that specific patterns can interfere with your efforts to support your child. Below, we've identified tendencies that inadvertently create self-doubt and a lack of confidence, inhibiting the development of a strong identity. Reflect on these and see where you recognize yourself. With increased awareness, you can begin making changes and transform your parenting approach.

Disapproval and Judgment

One day, 11-year-old Lara came into therapy looking tense. "I got these new pants with my birthday money." She sighed and plopped down onto the couch. "But Mom hurt my feelings. As we were about to leave, she went, 'That's what you're wearing? They're so baggy.' She's so judgy. I like them, but her comment made me feel bad about myself."

It bears repeating: what you say and do profoundly impacts how your child feels about themselves. Be careful what you say about their preferences. You might be sick of hearing their new favorite album, but if you snap, "What is this wretched noise? Turn it down!" they might interpret it as disliking something about them, not just about the artist blasting out of the speakers. And these beliefs last. You might mean, "I don't like this," and the child hears it as "I don't like you."

You should also steer clear of negative remarks about their bodies being too big or too small, too pale or too dark, or anything else that feels like a personal attack; hearing something like that from a parent is damaging. Even subtler comments sting. You might think it's innocuous to say, "That shirt's a little tight, honey," or "Why are you hungry again? You just ate!" But those nitpicks can impact kids' sense of self.

When we work with children, they often tell us they feel judged just for being the way they naturally are. Scrutiny can come from anywhere, and you can't change what will happen to them outside your doors. But what you can do is create a zone of safety where your child is always sure they can be themselves.

Rejection

Twelve-year-old Naomi, already sniffling, sat down and managed to say, "I told my mom that I have a crush on a girl, and she just said, 'Oh, you don't mean that. You're just copying something you heard at school.' I know she wouldn't say that if it was a boy." Naomi had been aware of her crushes on girls for a while and desperately wanted, and needed, her mom's acceptance.

Ten-year-old Connor mustered the courage to tell his mom at lunch one day that he was trans. "My mom was so mean about it, I wanted to die." We implore you to be open to what your kids have to say about their sexual orientation and gender identity, even if you don't understand it. When children feel like their parents don't accept who they are, they feel unlovable, ashamed, inherently bad, or even disgusting. What's more, peers (and insensitive adults) can be vicious and bullying. Children need you when they face adversity in the world, but they won't feel safe coming to you if you've rejected them. At critical moments like these, children rely on your unwavering support. Without it, their emotional distress and isolation dramatically increases, along with the risk of suicide, self-harm, and other mental health issues.

A study by the Trevor Project determined that almost half of LGBTQ+ youth ages 13 and up think seriously about taking their own lives. Nearly one in five transgender and nonbinary young people attempts suicide. Even higher rates are reported in communities of color. However, LGBTQ+ youth who received support from their families were much less likely to attempt taking their own lives.* We cannot express how important your role as a loving and supportive parent is for children.

Negative Labels

Too much criticism from parents creates constant pressure to live up to standards children can't meet, which makes them feel inadequate. These kids will hold themselves back from trying new things because of a blinding fear of making mistakes, and that can contribute to even higher anxiety levels because of the strong need to please you.

Little comments you might see as a joke or a throwaway can feel like a dart to the soul. Vanessa, a mother of three, says, "My stepdad always called me a klutz. To this day, when I make any minor mistake like accidentally knocking over something, I still feel bad about myself."

Comparing or labeling siblings in different ways can take a toll, too, such as saying, "Your sister is the academic one; you're the musical one." Never joke about who the favorite offspring is, and refrain from remarks like "That's such a classic middle-child thing to do." Comments that compare siblings can have a lasting negative impact on a child's self-perception.

---

*Trevor News, "The Trevor Project's Annual U.S. National Survey of LGBTQ Young People Underscores Negative Mental Health Impacts of Anti-LGBTQ Policies & Victimization," Trevor Project, May 1, 2023, https://www.thetrevor project.org/blog/the-trevor-projects-annual-u-s-national-survey-of-lgbtq -young-people-underscores-negative-mental-health-impacts-of-anti-lgbtq -policies-victimization.

Control

If you're a parent who tends to provide lots of hands-on help to your child, it might be time to take a step back. Even parents who know they're controlling find this difficult. One mom admitted, "I was helping my son decide on a charity project for his Sunday school, but I got too opinionated. He told me, 'Mom, let me breathe!' That hit home. I realized my 'helping' was actually suffocating him."

Most parents want to maintain control to ensure their child's safety and success in the world, but holding too tight a grip can backfire. While it might seem minor, there's a real link between children's anxiety and excessive parental interference. Kids who see their parents as overly involved often struggle to trust their own decisions, which can increase their worry and gradually undermine their self-esteem. Trust us, if you voice disapproval about your kid's choices—even one as innocuous as which charity they'd like to support—know that they're way more upset about letting you down (whether they can admit it or not) than about the actual decision they've made.

Resentment

Parents often tell us they are burned out, low on patience, and running on fumes. Chelsea said, "To be honest, I know my daughter can feel it when I am at the end of my rope. No joy, no patience—I'm embarrassed to say parenting just feels like an obligation right now." Just about everyone in the room nodded or said that they felt the same. Resentment is a normal feeling to have. Work these feelings out, either by talking them through with friends or seeing a counselor. Your kids know when you're "done" being a parent, and that takes a hit on their self-worth.

Self-Doubt and Lack of Confidence

Many parents find it tough to build a strong sense of self in their children simply because they didn't get much help in that department from their own parents. In these cases, confidence-building can feel like uncharted territory, and you might even step back, letting others who "click better" with your child lead the way. Sometimes, you might even feel envious watching your child prefer the company of other adults, or you may feel the sting of rejection, like one parent who shared, "I try to connect, but it's either an eye roll or a closed door. It's hard to know whether to approach or disappear."

Here's a quick tip: don't be discouraged if your child seems to shrug off some of your attempts to connect. For instance, imagine you're trying to talk about their day, and they're more interested in texting their friends. Instead of retreating with "Fine then, enjoy your phone," take a breath and plan a small joint activity, like making a snack together or going on some silly adventure. Simple, shared moments can often bridge gaps. Remember, a child's aloofness doesn't mean they don't need you. They do— more than they can sometimes show.

Kids are inherently programmed to bond with their parents; it's all about finding the right approach. When they push you away, that's when they need your presence the most, not to invade their space, but to gently remind them you're there, always ready to connect. Keep reaching out, even when it's tough. They're counting on you to guide the way.

* * *

Now that you know how big a role you play in your child developing a strong sense of self, let's look at some ways you can build them up.

Celebrate Your Child's Strengths, Interests, and Skills

Noticing and pointing out your child's unique strengths can help them internalize the message that they are great exactly as they are. That said, show them they are loved for existing, not for their clarinet-playing or talents on the robotics team. This reinforces the idea that their worth and value are not tied to performing well at school or coming in first in a competition, thus reducing the pressure for constant achievement. High expectations from parents often breed even higher anxiety and stress. Kids will still work hard! When they are valued by you simply for being themselves, their nervous systems can relax. One 9-year-old's parents told us that their son was feeling particularly bad about himself after his parents got his progress report. He said to his father, "Do you even love me?" to which his dad replied, "I have loved you from the moment you came into this world, and that will never change no matter what grades you get." It's vital for a child to feel that unconditional support that's not tied to outcomes, appearances, or performance.

Highlight Qualities

Be lavish about pointing out the qualities you admire in your kids, such as kindness, empathy, and creativity, by spotting and verbalizing them in the moment. It feels good to your kids (even if they play it cool) and your praise gets them excited about themselves. You don't need to go over-the-top, but acknowledging the positive traits or behaviors you notice via specific and meaningful comments is always a win.

If your child takes a clever approach to a problem, say so: "You're so good at working through friendship issues; you helped Declan talk to Andrés. How did you figure that out?" Talk about them to an adult when they are within earshot: "Wow, Kerry set up my phone for me so quickly, I'm really impressed." By noticing these strengths, you help them see the best parts of themselves.

One thing to keep in mind: It's common to praise your child only about the things that are important to you. For example, if hard work and intelligence have high value in your mind, you might miss that your child is the best organizer in the family, has a knack for making people laugh, or has an exceptional memory. See your kids for who they are and toss kudos their way like confetti throughout the week.

Nurture Their Interests

Encouraging your child to pursue their interests does more than just fill their time with fun—it actually boosts their happiness and reduces stress. When kids are involved in activities they love, they're fully engaged and naturally more relaxed. Help them explore these passions by signing up for classes they like, researching their favorite topics together online, reading books on subjects they're curious about, or learning about their favorite sports teams.

Aurora, age 10, for instance, loves thrifting. Although her mother doesn't always love her fashion choices, she's now beginning to see Aurora's emerging interest in sewing and told the group, "A year of fighting about what she wears, then yesterday I almost fell out of my seat when I connected the dots; she's just like my favorite great-granny Marie, who made clothes out of nothing!"

Even when your child talks nonstop about the same topic, there's always something more to discover. Remember an interest you lived for as a child and how much you cared about it. Look at the bigger picture and see what might be brewing in the background: a baseball enthusiast with a passion for player statistics might one day become a data analyst or a forensic accountant, and a kid who learns to rally players and direct campaigns for *Dungeons & Dragons* now can eventually lead large groups in any profession.

You might worry that your child's current passion seems immature, fearing they'll stick with it forever if you encourage them. But remember, their interests will evolve! By showing your kids how to wholeheartedly pursue what captivates them now, you're teaching them to dive deeply into different subject matters later on. There are Super Bowl champions and Supreme Court justices who did magic or played with sock puppets as kids.

Be Here Now

This is it! This is their one and only childhood. Showing up matters. Take twenty minutes to learn their favorite game once a week, even if you need a spreadsheet to keep track of the characters. Watch one of their TV shows together *without* your phone. Kids notice when you're half paying attention, and, yes, there may be a quiz after they share some ridiculous video clip they think is hilarious. Make it a habit to really be there for your kids—even when it's on their terms, not yours.

Be mindful and boost your child up. Listen to them talk about their card collection: really listen. "Which one is the most powerful? What does Snorlax do?"

Do all this even if what your child loves makes zero sense to you (hey, we had to Google what a Snorlax is, too!).

Your authentic and ongoing interest and attention is one of the most important resources in making your child feel seen and loved. Similarly, pay special attention to how your child fits into your family in terms of personality, interests, and skills. Sometimes, life winks at you, and your MMA-loving self winds up with a theater kid, and suddenly you're spending game day at a two p.m. musical matinee. The more you can cultivate what's important to them, the freer your child will feel to chart their own distinct course in life. As Tristan, who recently got into college on a full-ride math scholarship, told us, "My mom always laughs because she can't even figure out the tip on a restaurant check. She's an artist. But she and my stepmom didn't laugh when I asked to go to calculus camp, and they were in the front row at the mathematics Olympiad." In other words, seeing beyond your own interests as a parent can really add up.

Give Kids a Choice

Sometimes, you need to know when to pick your battles. We encourage you to let your child make decisions about who they want to invite over, what podcast they want to listen to on the way to school, and what style of clothing they choose to wear. As long as it's age-appropriate (or even pushing those numbers a bit), things will likely turn out fine. Encourage your children to decorate their walls with movie posters, their favorite photos, and other décor they like.

Be respectful—kids don't get to make a lot of decisions (since most things get decided by adults) and they need to feel like what they've picked out themselves is amazing. That's true even if you hate the nail polish color they choose or the death metal emanating from their room. Find something positive about what they're doing, even if it's "You're great at finding obscure bands!" If they are exploring their style and don't want to wear a holiday dress, don't force it on them just to please the grandparents (or yourself). Instead, appreciate that baggy pants or a wool hat in summer are expressive choices for them. Go with it rather than fighting when you can—they are figuring out their unique identity, and you get to be along for the wild ride.

Teach Basic Life Skills

Learning to do a grown-up task, like cooking, sewing, taking care of plants, or repairing something around the house gives a young person a sense of accomplishment and pride, which helps reduce worry. Kids want and need to learn what they are capable of, and this starts with small actions like feeding the meter after you park the car or calling the grocery store to find out if they have dill in stock for your soup recipe. Give your child more independence as they get older. This tells them they can trust themselves because you trust them, too.

A kid who can say, "I know how to do that!" is more apt to tackle difficult situations for the rest of their lives. Teach them practical skills like how to load the dishwasher or make an omelet (now we're talking lifelong skills!). Céline's twins have one big chore outside of cleaning their room each Saturday: Maxime washes their gym uniforms, and Claire folds them and puts them away. Children can balance negative thoughts about themselves with skills that help them feel confident—and you get some household benefits, too.

Be Open to Change

Prepare for your child's preferences to change regularly as they try on new likes and dislikes. Rather than criticizing them about how their interests seem to switch overnight ("You just told me you loved theme parks! Now they're not cool?"), go with what they're telling you now. Don't be the historian who says, "You just said last week that all you want to collect are Star Wars cards; now you want to collect insect exoskeletons!" Instead, tell your child, "I love that you have so many hobbies." Show them that loving them is easy, no matter what they're into—whether it's something unique or popular. This will reduce their worry, and they'll thank you later when they have a million eclectic interests.

Affirm Your Child's Gender and Sexuality

Children need their home to be a safe place where they can explore and express themselves as they begin to learn about their gender and sexuality. Instead of asking gendered questions, like "Which boys do you have crushes on?" try more open-ended ones, like "Who do you have a crush on? What do you want to wear that represents you?"

Your kid may tell you they're queer, transgender, nonbinary, or gender nonconforming. One parent in our group, Kayla, said, "My child told me from the age of four that she feels like a girl." Accept what they say is true to them. Let your child know that they have your unwavering love and support, even if you're still trying to understand everything or adapt to new or confusing information. This time of self-discovery is so delicate, and they need to feel emotionally safe to share their experiences with you.

They might not necessarily say these words but may show signs that they're not cisgender or heterosexual. Be loving and encouraging as they explore their identity. If they share a chosen name and pronouns, make every effort to use them. For example, Camilla, age 12, goes by they/them pronouns and says, "I'm so lucky to have a mom who uses my pronouns and lets me dress how I feel inside. Some days I might wear Doc Martens and my brother's wide brown leather belt with my hair slicked back. The next day I'll wear my pink and orange lace flower dress with silver sandals. I don't know what I would do without my mom, especially when kids and teachers won't use my pronouns."

Affirming your child's gender and sexuality openly is your way of respecting who they are, exactly as they are. It's how they feel safe. Be their advocate—speak up against transphobia and ensure that others respect their identity. Organizations like PFLAG, founded in the 1970s as the first and now largest entity dedicated to supporting, educating, and advocating for LGBTQ+ people and their families, are excellent resources to help you and your child navigate this path.

Keep Things Body Positive

You can help your child feel good about their body. Like every other part of building their self-esteem, this starts with you as their parent. State positively what our bodies can do and not what they look like. Encourage your child to appreciate themselves with affirmations like "Your body is so powerful; it helped you go on that long hike."

When you comment on other people's bodies, your child will fear that criticism coming their way, too. Instead, tell your child, "All bodies are different, and that's what's so cool about people."

Avoid complimenting your child for weight loss or body changes. Instead, celebrate self-expression: "I love the hair clips you picked out!" Tying self-esteem to appearances can be problematic, even with positive attention. They may fear losing your approval if their body changes in the future. Help them understand that their beauty shines through because of their true selves, not because of their body size.

Use Media to Empower

Introduce children to books, television series, and films that include diverse casts of characters, including Black and Brown families, queer and transgender individuals, and people of different body sizes. Choose media that mirror their experiences. When children see characters who look like them portrayed positively, it reinforces the message "There are people just like you!" This validation can raise their self-esteem and promote self-acceptance, which in turn reduces feelings of shame, anxiety, and depression. This isn't just to make media more enjoyable and relatable. Exposure to a wide range of characters can help children develop empathy and deeper understanding of others, including their siblings and classmates.

Bond with Your Child

Building a strong bond with your child isn't just for fun and friendship; your bond creates a protective barrier that acts like a force field, guarding them from feeling lonely and reducing stress. When kids feel close to you, they're also more likely to listen and learn from you. Think of your relationship as their home base, a safe place they can return to when things get tough.

Here are some ways you can strengthen your bond with your child.

Verbalize Your Love

Children need to hear from you how much you love them; it's not enough to assume they know. Pop your head into their room and remind them how important they are to you. Kids may laugh or scoff, but trust us, they need to hear those three magic words on a regular basis. Customize it to your child's interests: "I love you more than a scientist loves discovering a new planet." Show them you bought their favorite snack as you unload groceries and say, "Look! I saw this and thought of you."

If your child lights up receiving a casual compliment, say more. Tell them, "I like the color shirt you chose today. Blue looks so great on you." Or "I laugh so much when we spend time together. You're hilarious." Tell them you love them!

Leave Notes or Thoughtful Gifts

Leave a note on the mirror that says, "You're the coolest!" or just draw a smiley face and heart. Arjun loved the messages his dad would put in his lunch box every Friday. They were silly drawings he did on the fly that always included "XO, Dad." At the beginning of fourth grade, Arjun struggled to make friends; those notes would make him feel better when he felt sad during lunchtime.

Emily's foster family collected a stack of notes from her mom, and they opened one each Saturday over breakfast. Practicing shared parenting ensures that Emily can still feel close to and have reminders of her mother's love even while they are temporarily apart.

If you are traveling or live separately from your children during some part of the week, send them texts or emails and leave a voicemail, even if they don't pick up. When you return from a long trip, say, "I could not wait to see you. Look! I saw this souvenir rubber ducky with your name on it and just had to get it."

Make Them Your Be-All and End-All

You want your children to know they are your number-one priority. Give special attention to reunions with them—even in the morning and at the end of the day—to show your joy and enthusiasm in seeing them again. Talk sweetly to them if the moment is right, and tell them, with playfulness, "You'll always be my baby." Give them the first pick of the fortune cookies at the end of the meal and any spot they want on the couch.

If it's been a particularly tough day and one or both of you lost your cool, whisper something reassuring before bed: "Our relationship is so much more important than what happened between us today. Even when we argue, our connection never changes; you and your sister are always the most important people in the world to me."

Set Aside Mealtime Together

More than 1,500 research studies* show that frequent family meals have a positive effect on everything from body image to nutrition. Sitting down for meals regularly is known to reduce episodes of disordered eating, alcohol and substance use, violent behavior, and feelings of depression or thoughts of suicide in adolescents. These times have a straightforward task: connecting as a family as a regular part of everyday life, not as a special occasion.

Point Out Similarities

Talk about the positive ways that you and your child are similar. Emma's mom and her daughter say, "We both love making lists!

---

*Megan E. Harrison, "Systematic Review of the Effects of Family Meal Frequency on Psychosocial Outcomes in Youth," *Canadian Family Physician* 61, no. 2 (2015): 96–106, https://www.ncbi.nlm.nih.gov/pmc/articles/PMC4325878.

And if we had a snow day, we'd definitely go to the park because snow angels are our thing." Or share what you were like as a kid: "You love Taylor Swift. When I was your age, all I could think about was David Bowie. I had posters of him all around my room."

In the same way, identify parallels even when you don't have the same interests. For example, Roberto shared with the group that he overheard his daughter telling a friend, "Everyone says I have my nonna's eyes and my papa's sense of humor!" It was very sweet and put a smile on everyone's faces. When children have a unique way they connect to their caregivers, they feel their bond is special and important.

Mariah also shared, "I told my daughter I used to worry about friendships and school, too, and that sometimes I couldn't even fall sleep. I thought it might freak her out, knowing I worried when I was her age, but she said, 'Really, Mom?' and let out a big sigh. Even though she doesn't open up much to me these days, we had a great conversation."

Create a Special Gesture

Establishing a little sign that communicates "I'm here" can do wonders for lowering anxiety. Anya and her son will do three short squeezes on the hand, which stand for three words: "I. Love. You." She came up with this gesture when he was 5 years old, nervously awaiting a flu shot at the doctor's office, and it distracted and calmed him down. Now, at age 13, he returns it to her in times of stress as a silent way of checking in.

Bailey's dad gives her a wink in the rearview mirror when her carpool friends mention anything about throw-up; he knows it makes her anxious and his subtle acknowledgment helps a lot.

Spend Quality Time

Spend dedicated one-on-one time to establish a stronger bond with your child. The time you connect doesn't have to be long, but it does have to happen on a regular basis. Consistency is key. We understand finding and setting aside quality time can be challenging, but even twenty minutes a week can be a great start. Being present with each other helps soothe both of your nervous systems, so pick an activity you enjoy and let those few minutes with them fill you with wonder and awe.

Here are some ideas for how to spend quality time with your child:

• **Do a creative project:** Help them redecorate their room or make a photo collage above their bedside table. Get out the markers, even if all you can draw are weird cats and stick figures. Help them with a project they're passionate about, like building the longest cascade of dominoes they can or taking apart old electronics to craft futuristic sculptures.

• **Prepare a dish:** As Jasmine told us, "We love to cook, so every week my eldest and I pick out a recipe to make together for Sunday brunch. Messy as it always is to clean up, I love this special time with him."

• **Sit side by side:** Some children prefer to sit beside their caregiver. Read or journal on the same couch. Nolan's family loves puzzles, so they like to work on one at the living room table.

- **Get active:** Arm-wrestle or go for brisk walks after dinner. Play catch, and don't worry if you're not super athletic. Jermaine told us, "I'd always deferred sports to my wife because she played lacrosse in college, but my kids don't care about my skill level."

Show Physical Affection

Elizabeth and her wife were working on finding ways to connect with their child in session one afternoon, when she said, "My parents hardly ever hugged me, so showing affection is pretty unfamiliar to me. I was nervous to try it, but as awkward as I feel, both kids are beginning to respond to it. Some weeks later, Isaac came into our room and asked if he could get in my side of the bed and cuddle. I was really excited because that's never happened before."

Some kids like head scratches before bed or an arm around their shoulder during a movie. Cuddling may not be everyone's thing and some kids won't be receptive to this kind of connection. Make sure your children know they're in charge when it comes to their body by letting them define their own comfort levels.

Ask them if they are comfortable with it first: "Can I hug you?" It's fine if your child prefers a wave goodbye or a fist bump instead of a kiss. Everyone has different preferences, and those can change over time. In fact, kids tend to need more personal space as they get older, and it's essential to teach them that they can say no if they don't want physical contact. When you respect your child's "no's," you practice consent with them and empower them to confidently assert their boundaries in interactions with others. Let your child know you will have their back when they ask their cousin not to roughhouse so hard with them.

Cultivate a Sense of Belonging to Something Bigger

As we wrap up this chapter, let's look at skills to enhance your child's identity through their family history, sense of community, and broader culture.

Tell Family Stories

The more children know about their family history, the more grounded they feel. A fascinating Emory University research study, known as the "Family Narratives Project," showed that knowing details such as where their parents and grandparents grew up and what jobs they had gave children a stronger sense of control over their own lives and higher self-esteem.[*]

Tell your child about the different members of your family and draw a family tree to help them visualize each link. Start today. Say, "Do you know what I do for work? What about Grandma?" If they don't know, have fun telling them.

Pass down wisdom and stories, making it fun and age-appropriate. Claudia from our parent group shared, "Now that I think about it, my kids are mesmerized by my dad's stories of

---

[*] "Family Narratives," Family Narratives Lab, Emory University, https://scholar blogs.emory.edu/familynarrativeslab/family-narratives.

immigrating to America and how he and his siblings each had to choose just one toy to bring with them when they fled Guatemala. He kept his shaggy, one-eyed lion cub for all these years and brought it on his latest visit to show the kids."

Talk about funny anecdotes from when your child was a baby and show them pictures. Share how you felt when they were born and who else couldn't wait to meet them. Tell and retell stories as they grow older. Children are visual learners; watch old videos and have keepsakes and photographs of family members around. Show your child what you have saved from the past and explain why.

Pass Down Heirlooms

Ellie came into therapy one day with a jade necklace on. She shared excitedly that it had been her mom's, but she got it for her eighth birthday the previous weekend. She touched it proudly, saying she wanted to give it to her own daughter one day.

If you don't have tangible objects to pass down, think of a recipe or a hobby that unites you with a member of your family. Eleven-year-old Luis learned to fingerpick on the family's flamenco guitar, just like his tía, and beams with pride when his mom says the music reminds her of her childhood.

If you don't feel connected to your family history, find another thread to pull from the past to help your child feel pride and connection to a bigger community. Maybe you are rooted in the history of your town or city. Gavin, a 9-year-old New Yorker, likes to share, "We're from Manhattan. This borough used to be completely covered in grass. We had the first-ever pizzeria in America, and there's something in the water that gives us the best bagels."

The Power of "Weak Ties"

Beyond the immediate household, there are countless people most families interact with on a casual basis, from neighbors and religious congregants to near-strangers you encounter at skate parks, cultural festivals, parades, and markets. Psychologists call these types of connections "weak ties" or "peripheral ties" to distinguish them from close family and intimate friends. You might just call it "community." The people who cross our paths are important. Their presence is good for our moods and our health, and for feeling less isolated. Help your kids see the people around them as allies and friends you haven't yet met. Join block parties, spend time with extended relatives, introduce your kids to friends you knew back when. Reinforcing these relationships shows a child how important they are to the people around them. After having dinner with her best friend of twenty years, Neyana told her daughter, "Kiara told me she loves to do origami with you and can't wait to see what the next one will be." Kids look back and remember who spent time paying attention to them.

Encourage Social Groups

Being a valued team member gives kids community and a sense of purpose as they contribute, take on responsibilities, and make decisions. School is an excellent place for kids to expand their social networks. Leah casually connects with other fifth graders in the after-school garden club, at the junior science fair, and in the library helpers' group. Ernesto's stepdad laughs and says,

"My son has a much more active social life than I do. Tomorrow he's got New Friend Day and next week he's doing Peer Reading Buddies. He's always saying his favorite part of school isn't the school part; it's the people part." Being part of a group that meets weekly in a structured format also gives children a sense of stability, and knowing their role in a group helps strengthen their sense of independence. Blake, age 11, says, "I love being a theater techie. It's my life! We get to wear black, my favorite color, and I always do all the lighting by myself. After the last show, we drink Diet Coke through our Twizzlers. Don't tell my parents!"

Connect to Cultural Identity

At some point—perhaps it's happened already—your children will notice that things aren't fair, and that some people get special treatment and have more opportunities because of their appearance. Experiencing prejudice significantly influences how children perceive themselves and their place in the world. That's why a strong sense of belonging is necessary. Connecting with others who share their similar traits helps children stand firm in the face of the hurtful things others may say or do.

Surround your child with people who share their ethnicity, values, or cultural background. Identity-based groups can provide a safe space for kids to be themselves. Jackson was a member of their school's Black Student Union, Rania was the president of the LGBTQ+ Alliance student group, and Kaito went to Japanese classes on Sundays. Let your child feel the power of a collective, where they can find confidence and pride in themselves rather than believe society's faulty messages that put them down.

Establish Traditions

Traditions are more than just routines we engage in for the holidays; they carry meaning, create a sense of togetherness, amplify joy, and help your child build understanding of who they are. They can be big or small. What sets them apart is the thoughtfulness and purpose behind them. When you repeat them consistently, they become memorable and eventually nostalgic.

Participating in religious or cultural practices can also create a sense of belonging while drawing out a sense of pride. Pedro, who is Dominican, said, "On Nochebuena, which is Christmas Eve, my family would party all night. A lot of bachata and merengue. Learning the dances for me felt like I was honoring my tradition and my heritage. Even in college, I was part of the campus Latin Dance group."

Some cultures have a rite of passage that marks the transition from childhood to adulthood, like a Bahra ceremony in the Newah community of Nepal, bar mitzvahs and bat mitzvahs in Jewish tradition, and quinceañeras in Mexican and other Latin American cultures. Identify what traditions you want to commemorate, then figure out what you can instill with more intentionality. Tell your children about the ceremonies, where they started, and why.

Traditions can also look like celebrating your family members. During dinner, honor milestones and talk about why you are marking the occasion. Do it more often than you think you should! "Today, we are celebrating Christian's finishing a super-complicated radio-controlled-airplane set he's been working on for months but wanted to give up on several times. We are so proud of you for sticking with it until you got it built."

Start new family traditions. Ever since his youngest was 6 years old, Dad wakes up whoever is having a birthday and takes them to get fresh donuts from the store at six a.m. They eat one there together and bring more home for the family. Now, everyone looks forward to birthday donuts.

* * *

Remind your child how much you love them in big and small ways, spend time together, and build up their interests. The close bond you create with them goes a long way in helping them feel good about themselves and ward off stress. And when the world goes haywire, or someone insults them at school, they know they have you.

For those of you for whom this type of parent-child bond is vastly different from your relationship with your parents, lean into that special knowing that you get to give your child an experience you didn't have. You never know; taking this approach may heal a little bit of your inner child, too.

Questions and Reflections
for Deeper Thinking

Here's another chance to delve deeper into the relationships that shape your child's world—including friends, family, and community—and how these relationships impact their self-perception. Really reflect on the stressors they might face at school or with peers, like feeling out of place or dealing with bullying. The more you understand your child's experience in the world, the better you can support and protect them.

- How does your child feel they fit in with family, friends, and others around them? Name some places where they feel a strong sense of belonging. Are there specific instances when they feel "different," or social settings that contribute to their anxiety?

- How would you describe your bond with your child? What might your child say about it? What steps can you take right now to strengthen this connection?

- Reflect on when you may have found it challenging to fully accept aspects of your child's identity or choices. How can you work toward offering unconditional love and support, especially in areas where you might have different views or experiences?

- What positive qualities does your child see in themselves? How do they think others view them? What traits can you highlight to help build a positive self-narrative?

- Do you have any reservations about discussing your heritage or continuing family traditions? What new ones could you start?

Six

Engage Like a Pro

"When I was pregnant," Ana said, "I imagined being a mom and having a close relationship with my daughter. I pictured us chatting about everything from science (my great love) to makeup. Sadly, our conversations now are mostly about logistics, and when I try to get her to open up, I get nowhere."

Parents often ask us how to better communicate with their children, particularly when conversations fall flat or feel one-sided. Engaging like a pro allows you to have deeper conversations, learn more about your children's experiences, and help keep them safe. When you respond to your child in a way that works for them, they're more likely to want to share even more of their inner world with you.

This step is the remedy to a critical concern that parents repeatedly bring to us, like Khaled, who said, "My child gets frustrated when I ask him about school or friends and always tells me, 'Dad, stop asking me so many questions.'"

To be clear, Engage Like a Pro doesn't mean you should sound like a know-it-all in front of your kids. Rather, it's about learning how to talk to your kids in a way that makes them feel heard and safe so they'll want to open up more about what they're feeling and experiencing. This approach is how professional therapists like us help caregivers find deeper and more meaningful connections with their children.

The strategies in this chapter will help you build a direct line of communication with them to support them now and through their teenage years. The more connected conversations you have, the more likely they are to return to you to share their thoughts and feelings and get your guidance—a significant factor in helping lower anxiety. Let's look at a mom practicing SAFER Parenting to see how these exchanges can go with the tools you will learn in this chapter.

Grace was 12 years old when Mom told us the story: "My sweet angel sat on the bus stressing out that I'd get mad if she brought up drugs," she said. "Let's be honest. I felt like crawling into a hole when she did, but I'm so glad she came to me."

Grace: "Mom, can we talk about something?"

Mom: "Of course. What's on your mind?"

Grace: "Promise you won't be mad at me."

Mom: "I'm here to listen, sweetie."

Grace: "Well, you know Addison, my friend, right? She and some other kids were talking about ecstasy at lunch. I kept hearing about scary stuff, like, maybe you could see things that aren't really there. But it's not like I'm going to do drugs."

Mom: "I can understand why that would sound scary."

Grace: "I want to be included in the conversation, but I'm

afraid they'll figure out that I don't know what I'm talking about."

Mom: "That's a lot to think about, wanting to be included and being afraid at the same time."

Grace: "Yeah, like, I don't want to sound clueless to my friends."

Mom: "Maybe you're a little worried about peer pressure?"

Grace: "Yeah, a little. When they talk about it, it feels like they have their own secrets and jokes, and sometimes I'm not part of it, and I do want to be part of it, but I don't. It's confusing."

Mom: "Hmm . . . sounds like you're feeling a bit excluded, and it's uncomfortable to hear them talk about drugs? I understand why this might feel tough."

Grace: "Yeah, it's so weird. But I need to do homework. Can we talk more later?"

Mom: "Always, kiddo. Thanks for sharing with me."

As you can imagine, Grace's mom was beyond eager to start educating her child about the dangers of ecstasy. However, shifting into lecturing mode while a child is sharing something important could result in losing their engagement in the conversation. Moving too quickly to a protective position can discourage your child from being as open with you in the future. This mom understood that rushing into a teaching moment could stop the conversation, and her goal was to get as much sharing going as she could. She followed Grace's cue to pause when her daughter needed a break from the conversation.

Mom holds back from saying, "Don't do drugs," or explaining the dangers. She's been honing this skill with us and trusted she could educate her daughter later. So, the next day, after school, she said to her daughter, "I want to tell you more about ecstasy. It's not safe, and here's why," and explained it calmly and left room for questions. She's a better "coach" to her daughter, and Grace is always more receptive, even a day later.

Daniel, age 10, on the other hand, was quite the opposite, although his parents told us how open they were with their son. He said, "My mom thinks we're close, but here are all the things I'm not telling her . . ." We learned that his parents tended to underreact or overreact, so he simply started sharing less and less.

As therapists and parent coaches, we see people reveal everything under the sun in our offices. When we hear something shocking, we don't say, "Oh my god," or "You did WHAT?" We stay collected and listen with curiosity—no matter what. We know that people will say a lot more if we don't have a big reaction.

When your children talk with you regularly, you can recognize trouble and distress signs faster. Engaging like a pro cultivates a powerful parent-child connection, showing them they can navigate life changes *with* you. Most important, you will be able to address worries promptly and help prevent them from escalating.

Roadblocks to Engaging Like a Pro

When kids share, many parents try to fix the problem, minimize their child's big feelings, or escalate by maximizing the situation. Picture the caretaker running over to a child in meltdown mode, offering a singsong "You're fine, you're fine, you're fine" without even knowing what's wrong. These responses may be genuine attempts to support your child, but they are not helpful and can sometimes have the opposite impact.

Let's look at each through the lens of Oliver's story.

Still sweaty from playing flag football with friends after school, Oliver, age 7, slumped on the couch and cried to Mom, "My friend Ryan wouldn't even let me play. Then he pushed Omar, which really made me mad, so I ran over and ripped off his flag." At this point, his eyes were welling up, and his mom could tell he was getting upset. He cleared his throat, looked at her sadly, and said, "The coach kicked me out of the game, but Ryan should have been kicked out, not me!"

Fixing: The Rescuers

Faster than a child can say, "Uh-oh," these parents are the fix-it fairies, using their pixie dust to spray solutions all over the situation. A parent with this tendency might be inclined to jump in and say, "Well, the next time this happens, you should tell the coach immediately how you feel. And be sure to tell Ryan not to push Omar anymore."

It's natural to want to resolve your child's dilemma by suggesting a solution. When your child's feelings are hurt, it may feel like yours have been injured, too. But going straight to problem-solving or giving resolutions too soon will leave your child feeling as though their emotions have been overlooked.

When falling into this mode, a parent anxiously reacts by throwing directives: "You need to march up to the coach tomorrow and tell them exactly what happened," or "Write an apology note right now." Peppering them with recommendations or concerns too soon makes children feel bulldozed, discouraged, and nervous to tell you how they feel next time. They may not bring it up again.

That's why it's vital to avoid presenting other positions initially. Be on their side even if you feel tempted to suggest another perspective. Skip "Hmm, I think your coach is actually right because . . ." as it will indicate you are not aligned with your child. And be sure to keep a keen eye out for questioning their motives while telling a story. Challenges like "But why'd you rip his flag off if you know you're not supposed to?" can end up feeling more critical than helpful.

Kids often tell us, "My parents start telling me what to do instead of just listening." If you tend toward wanting to correct the situation, consider whether your parents might have done the same in your childhood. Even with the best intentions to "do it differently," we can easily fall into familiar patterns.

Minimizing: The Downplayers

Sometimes, parents can make too little of a situation a child shares, often done unconsciously to end the conversation. It sounds like this: "Don't worry about what the coach did; it's not a big deal. It's none of your business." Or "You'll be fine," and "I'm sure nothing will come of it; just forget it." This is the problem-solving parent equivalent of a "skip" button; it implies, "Why bother with the issue at hand when you can just fast-forward to the 'important' part?"

Your intention may be to prepare your children to have grit and not make a big deal about things, but making too little of their feelings sends the message that their thoughts and emotions are not as meaningful as they think they are.

Minimizing can be habitual if you grew up in a family that didn't pay attention to your feelings. So, watch for messages to your children like "Stop crying," "That's ridiculous," "Toughen up," "That's no big deal," "I was only joking," or "That's nothing for you to worry about!" These comments can significantly increase anxiety and may lead to feelings of humiliation in your child. As a result, they may hesitate to speak with you in the future, fearing that their concerns will seem insignificant at best, and ridiculous at worst.

Ultimately, children with parents who minimize may become adults who undervalue their needs in relationships with others.

Maximizing: The Amplifiers

You don't need a cannon to kill a mosquito, and you don't need to go overboard with your reactions to every little mishap. Overreacting can make kids feel like their problems are too intense even for adults to handle.

Hearing about the game, Oliver's mom reacts strongly. "This is absolutely unacceptable! I can't believe they would treat you like this. We need to sort this out right now!" She picks up her phone, her voice loud and tense, and starts calling other parents to rally support. "We're going to make sure everyone knows about this and that it never happens again!" Oliver watches her pace back and forth, feeling his initial upset morphing into a major ordeal. This heightened reaction increases the intensity of the situation, overwhelming him and making him anxious about future interactions at school and sports.

As parents, you're maximizing when you say, "Get down here and clean this up before our guests arrive! This is so embarrassing!" when you see a pile of homework that wasn't cleared from the table. A maximizer will dub it a "crisis" when they discover a child has used up all the printer ink or left a small stain on a new carpet. "Everything's ruined now!" you might say. But is it really?

When your child comes to you with upsetting news or emotions, don't jump on the big-emotions bandwagon. Reacting in overblown ways demonstrates to your child that you can't keep them safe in their emotions because you, too, have significant feelings to attend to. Your child needs you to stay steady and not make more of what may already be a stressful situation for them.

Pop Quiz

Imagine a parent is in the kitchen making dinner when her child walks in and says, "Track was awful today. I finished half a second behind my last sprint time." Which of the following responses is an example of fixing, which is minimizing, and which is maximizing?

1. "I'm sure you did fine. Go wash up for dinner."

2. "What do you mean you think you didn't beat your time? We have been working on it for weeks!"

3. "Immediately after dinner, email your coach to see what you can do to make up for today's practice."

Answers: 1. Minimizing, 2. Maximizing, 3. Fixing

Sarcasm

Despite your best intentions, making sarcastic remarks can often hurt your child's feelings. Therefore, it's necessary to take what kids say seriously and be on the lookout for sarcasm, even when used jokingly. Marissa, a single mom, told us, "My mom would say things like 'Oh, is that a new hairstyle called "Don't Brush It at All"?' I know she was trying to be funny, but looking back, it really hurt my feelings."

Accusations

Children also need to feel their voices and ideas are essential in a conversation. You might be tempted to say, "Your point doesn't even make sense!" Be open to their ideas and help them think through things while showing them kindness. Watch out for hasty accusations: if you hear information about them from someone else, start by giving your child the benefit of the doubt. Get their perspective first.

Also, be careful of coming off as disapproving. As soon as you cue that you are skeptical, kids are likely to zip up and take their thoughts and feelings underground, which can ultimately be a significant source of anxiety.

Guilt

When Derek started in an afternoon parenting group, he told us about a conversation with his 11-year-old where he got upset and said, "You never talk to me. How come your friend Kofi tells his dad about Mock Trial, and you don't?" He said he immediately wanted to take the words back, as he'd sounded just like his mother.

The truth is, we learn our communication styles from somewhere, usually our parents. Most everyone has heard of a guilt trip, which is an emotional manipulation to make the person feel bad and ultimately influence their behavior or decision. We hear this from many parents who feel frustrated at the lack of communication from their children, get impatient with the process, and the words of blame just pour out.

Children need the repetition of many successful conversations with you in order to want to have more of them. In the therapy room, we exhibit tremendous patience when waiting for someone to open up about their deepest thoughts and feelings; we don't force it. Sometimes, it takes months. Eventually, with enough emotional safety, it happens. If you feel exasperated by your child's silence and want to play the guilt card, remember that flowers bloom in a garden when they are nurtured over time, not because they are coerced into blossoming. Guilt-tripping makes kids fear disappointing others, consequently raising anxiety levels and creating a sense of emotional pressure and inadequacy.

• • •

Now that you are clear about what to avoid when engaging and communicating with your child, let's consider how to have talks like a pro.

How to Engage Like a Pro

To have meaningful conversations where children feel comfortable sharing their innermost thoughts and feelings, tailor the way you communicate with them. Children engage in dialogue differently than adults do, requiring special consideration and trust to open up. Here, we share everything you need to know about engaging like a pro.

Approach Carefully

Our colleague has a cat named Diesel, a fourteen-pound, blue-eyed Ragdoll. He's a real beauty but afraid of his shadow and almost every sound he hears. He will be your friend, though it takes time. If you rush toward him, he'll run under the bed and will not reappear until all humans who don't live in his home leave.

Some kids are a lot like Diesel when it comes to having conversations. They will only talk if they feel the conditions around them are safe. If you interrupt them or come in with a barrage of questions, or sometimes even one, they will get overwhelmed, feel embarrassed, and run away or close off.

For example, when you see your kid after school, it's very tempting to start asking, "How was school? Who did you sit with? What did you learn in class?" But most parents say they get one-word answers that leave them sorely disappointed and their children annoyed. As much as you are eager to connect, moving quickly toward a child with this sort of pace is usually going to be met with rejection.

Keep It Casual

Instead, foster an environment where your child will be more naturally inclined to confide in you. Aim for laid-back, open-ended conversations, except when discussing serious issues like personal safety, family expectations, or school-related matters.

Think about chatting in unexpected places, like the kitchen or when you are driving and they are in the backseat. Generally, kids don't want to sit across from you and have deep talks. So, strike up a conversation in the car or take a walk down the street instead. They'll be able to hear you but won't have to look right at you, which can feel like less pressure.

Observe where your child naturally becomes more communicative and spend more time in those settings. Bao, age 8, loves to do pastels on her sketch pad on the floor of the living room. She doesn't care if her dad sits on the couch and does the day's crossword puzzle. She will open up in that setting.

Put Your Things Down

To engage with your child like a pro, get fully present and ready to listen. Be curious and interested in what they have to say. Show them you care by setting your phone or laptop aside. You will get miles further if you aren't staring at your screen.

Talk to Them with Respect

Avoid using a baby voice when talking to your child; instead, address them with a warm, genuine tone. Speaking naturally conveys respect for their growing maturity and intelligence, recognizing them as evolving individuals worthy of sincere interaction. Steer clear of dismissive remarks such as "Well, you don't know yet because you're too young."

Twelve-year-old Elijah told us he grew out of the word "daddy" and felt embarrassed when his mom kept using it when she referred to him, even when the boy's friends were present. "Somehow 'dad' feels less babyish, and it makes me want to scream that my mother can't get her head around that," he said.

Be open-minded, consider their new and different viewpoints, and give space to new philosophies. Show that you value what they think and feel, letting them experience themselves as someone with cool thoughts and ideas.

Offer Comfort

Some children appreciate physical touch while sharing. Ask if they'd like a hug, to hold your hand, or simply to have you sit next to them. Others prefer not to be touched in these moments and might appreciate it if you hand them a fidget toy or something else to occupy their hands.

Allow for Breaks

Respect your child's pace and notice if they're shutting down on a conversation. They might appear antsy, change the subject, or start humming. Let it drop and say, "We can talk about it later."

We do the same thing in our work as therapists and pause a topic until the next session because everyone can benefit from a break in unpacking feelings.

When You Can't Talk Right Now, Let Them Know You Care

If you're unable to have a conversation with your child immediately, it's important to communicate your interest and care. There will be many times when you're otherwise occupied, speaking with someone else, or need to attend to work. It's fine to postpone a conversation, but make sure your child knows you value what they have to say. You might try, "I really want to hear what happened in your class today. Can we talk about it after dinner? I want to give you my full attention, but right now, I'm still on the clock."

Let Them Talk (and Talk and Talk)

Everyone needs a place to let it all out. So, when your child is venting, don't stop the flow. Look them in the eyes. Nod. Say "mm-hmm." Be genuine. Rather than trying to direct every conversation or force them to respond to a rat-tat-tat of questions, leave things open-ended. You'll get better results with lines like "Tell me more about that," or "What happened next?" These simple phrases are sometimes all a child needs to keep talking. Give them space and attention and watch the conversation flow.

Sometimes, children share something that makes you feel scared, hurt, or concerned. In these moments, play it cool, even if it makes your hair stand on end. If your kid tells you the wildest thing, respond as if they just told you they had grilled cheese for lunch. If not, they'll think, "Don't tell Dad things like this in the future," or "Yaya doesn't like this about me. I better not share anymore." Better to go quiet and drop your nuggets of wisdom at the end of the conversation or another time.

Make Space for Rants

Abigail, age 10, doesn't need help starting conversations. Sometimes, she needs help reining it in because she's given to rants. A typical opening line as she hops into the backseat at school pickup: "Mom, Mr. Jenkins is so, so rude. I mean, he doesn't even listen to anyone! Nobody! He's so weird. I can't stand him! I hate his class! I can't believe we have to take this test tomorrow. He's so crazy . . ." and so on, ad infinitum.

Even if it comes across as negative, this type of chatter isn't necessarily bad. It's Abigail's way of venting, and her mom knows to just let her talk. Keep this in mind if you have an expressive young talker in the family. Just because kids are on a tear about something doesn't mean they won't figure their way through complicated feelings. A word waterfall like that is usually a way kids get their initial thoughts out in the open. Let it pour.

It's tempting to respond to every complaint or confession when they vent, but if you intervene too soon—especially with criticism or suggestions—they may not have the chance to fully express what they're feeling. If they sense your disapproval, they may feel ashamed that they had any of these thoughts in the first place.

If you want to be their confidant, let their initial feelings come out raw. We liken it to writing a rough draft before submitting a final paper. It takes a moment before they figure out how they really feel.

We know Mom doesn't want Abigail to despise her teacher. Just because kids are negative about something now doesn't mean they won't see it differently later. They're more likely to stay open to ideas when parents listen to all their thoughts and feelings first.

If Mom hadn't handled it well, she might have said, "Come on, science is important. Don't talk about your teacher that way." But instead, Mom made a mental note to discuss calling people words like "weird" or "crazy" another time so she could focus on her daughter's feelings first. She tapped into her SAFER Parenting skills and said, "Mr. Jenkins got on your nerves today, huh? Sounds like science class was tough."

Abigail looked up gloomily and said, "Nicholas said my school project was ugly." Mom realized her daughter was actually feeling embarrassed and hurt by her classmate, not really by science or Mr. Jenkins.

After letting Abigail get her feelings off her chest, Mom understood what was really bothering her. Later, when Abigail was calmer, Mom came back around to discuss kind language.

Sidestep "Always" and "Never"

Children often use "always" and "never" to express strong emotions, even if every situation, as we grown-ups know, comes with a thousand nuances.

Ali shared in a group session that whenever his daughter Derya, age 9, talked about her YMCA class, she would say she's "never going back" and that it was "the worst class ever." Initially, Dad would counter these statements firmly, reminding his daughter that the class was paid for and she was expected to attend, which invariably led to arguments.

It took a while to realize that Derya's relationship with words like "always" and "never" had more to do with frustration than literal truth. So, Dad changed his approach. Instead of disputing Derya's absolute terms, he began acknowledging his daughter's feelings by saying things like "It sounds like today was really tough. What happened in class?" This shift in response helped them avoid constant battles and led to more open, productive conversations.

Understanding that children often use "always" and "never" as a release valve can help you address the emotions behind the words, facilitating better communication and reducing conflicts.

Count Down to Hear More

Through many years of working with children, we've learned that they process and articulate thoughts more slowly than adults. So, give them plenty of time to find the words they want to use.

After you speak, count down slowly from ten to zero (we have liftoff!) before adding anything more; it's a way to avoid the urge to fill the silence. Allow quiet spaces and let them take their time to respond. Therapists have long recognized that by staying quiet, you allow the other person to express more, and they will.

Children may repeat themselves frequently as they sort out their feelings. Make sure to let them complete their thoughts before drawing any conclusions. Be patient; you will likely be rewarded with surprising insights from their responses.

Echo

Echoing is a communication tool where you paraphrase what your child shares. This practice works in psychotherapy rooms worldwide because there is something comforting about hearing your ideas come back and knowing you are heard. It helps children think through different scenarios on their own, which strengthens their problem-solving skills. They learn what they like and what sets them off by talking out loud with you. In turn, they develop higher emotional intelligence and become naturally calmer because when they are sure someone understands them, they feel safe in that person's presence.

Here's how to echo with your child: After they speak, say back what you heard in your own words, letting them know you understood them. Keep the main plot but use different words. Use inflection in your tone like you're in it with your child, and rather than parroting it back—which will likely tick them off— rephrase it slightly. Don't worry if this doesn't come naturally— you will become a pro as you practice!

Let's look at an example of echoing in action. James shared with our parenting group, "I tried echoing last night. My eleven-year-old said, 'Life is so unfair,' a phrase I really dislike. But I echoed, 'Life's unfair, huh?' To my surprise, he opened up and said, 'Tyler wouldn't let me sit where I wanted on the bus. It made me so mad, Dad.'

"I couldn't believe he was talking to me, so I echoed more: 'Oh man, Tyler was a jerk to you today. I understand how that made you mad.'

"He said, 'Yeah. I'll just start sitting with Robin on the bus instead.'

"Even though internally I was screaming, 'But he's your best friend! You've known him your whole life, and I've known his parents since high school; you can't not be friends!' I heard you two in my head and instead said, 'It must have been really hard on you today if you don't want to ride with him to school any-more.'

"He said, 'Yeah, Dad, it is. Thanks for getting it.' I almost fell off the bed! Here's the best part—they were friends again in less than twenty-four hours, and all by allowing his feelings and echoing them, we didn't fight."

When they sadly say, "I am not as smart as the other kids in the class!" you aren't going to excitedly echo back, "Of course, you're not as smart!" Sigh naturally and say, "Yeah, you're com-paring your Spanish scores, and you're not feeling as smart as the other kids." When they fly into the room screeching, "I got the part in the play!" echo what you are seeing and hearing by saying excitedly, "You got the part you wanted!"

Listening can be tougher than fixing things, especially when your child is upset. Echoing their feelings gives you something to work with. A mom in our group explained her daughter's frustration after being dress-coded at school for her early developing body, which led to a humiliating moment. "They made me wear a school sweatshirt from lost and found to cover up my boobs." The mom knew her daughter felt terrible. Her daughter is tall for her age and already sensitive about standing out. Instead of trying to soothe her with compliments about how beautiful her body is (and risk getting eye rolls), the mom decided to simply echo her daughter's feelings: "That sounds really embarrassing and frustrating." Her daughter responded, "Exactly, Mom. I just don't want to stand out because of my body."

Parents often tell us, "I've tried to echo what he says, and my kid hates it." Be sure you're changing what you say enough that they don't feel like you're a parental parrot. A child can take a minute to get used to it, and you should be transparent. Tell them you've learned a new way to communicate, allowing the other person to just say what's on their mind. Tell them you don't mean to annoy them but wish to understand their thoughts and feelings before you jump in and help. Take it slow, and you will get into a groove. You can even teach it to them and ask if they'd like to try echoing you. Have fun with it; this is an opportunity for you to be light and playful as you try out this skill.

Ask What They Want

Sometimes, conversations are hard because your child is angry with you, and you may feel like these tools don't work at all. You may be into a conversation, echoing, validating, and listening to them, and they're frustrated and hate it, maybe even snapping, "Stop doing that!" and nothing seems to change the situation. So, when in doubt, ask what they want from the conversation. In relationships, what's most important is attempting to get it right.

Ask your child the special question: "Do you want my opinion or for me to just be on your team and listen?" If they don't know what they need, take a break and help them turn to a coping tool. Come back to the conversation when everyone feels better.

Pause on Advice (Sometimes)

If they ask for advice, that's one thing. But parenting isn't simple, and sometimes advice is the opposite of what your kid wants in the moment. It's only natural to come up with solutions to a problem your child is expressing. But if they're not looking for a fix, your brilliant input can spike resentment or irritation, because a child can think, "You never think I have good ideas—I know that already!" Often, what kids really need is a listening ear.

Let them talk through the situation and possible solutions first. In our parenting circles, we always do this (contrary to popular belief, therapists don't just dole out advice!).

Here's how things might go if you give kids the space to find their own way through a situation:

Peter, age 10, talked about how his sister was number one on his no-invite list for his trampoline party in two weeks. She had pushed him too far. He exclaimed to the whole family, "She can't come! I don't ever want to see her again." This was tricky since there was no chance she was skipping the party, but Peter's halmoni, Korean for grandmother, knew she needed to let him talk it out at a quieter moment. Pay close attention to how Halmoni echoes while well aware that Peter will have to come to terms with his sister attending the party.

As Peter sat on the living room floor building Legos, with Halmoni on the couch, he had the space to talk about his frustration and anger.

Peter: "My sister's the worst. She won't leave me and my friends alone. It's embarrassing."

Halmoni: "You can't escape her, huh?"

Peter: "NO! And I have to share a room with her! She's going to ruin my party if she comes."

Halmoni: "You're worried she'll get in the way, like she does when we paint together?"

Peter: "Yeah, I told Mom already that she can't come."

Halmoni: "What did she say?"

Peter: "That I have to invite her."

Halmoni: "Aw, darn—she said you have to, huh?"

Peter: "Yeah, and she always gets to come. It's not fair."

Halmoni: "The life of a big brother isn't fair."

Peter: "Yeah."

Halmoni: "Ugh, well, we know she has to come. What do you think it'll be like when she's there?"

Peter: "Awful, but her friend is coming, so they'll probably just hang out with each other."

Halmoni: "So, she'll be doing her own thing."

Peter: "Yeah, probably."

Take note of how Peter had the solution the whole time. He just needed a little space to get there. Children sometimes need you to help them with advice or solutions, but check to see if they can figure it out first. Giving your child this opportunity allows them to learn critical problem-solving tools that help them manage emotions.

If they press you to tell them what you think, be sure you address what they need help with, not what you want to teach them. So, if Mia asks her mom for advice about getting her friend in first grade to trade Skittles for her banana at lunch and Mom says, "You know Skittles are bad for you and you won't be able to learn if you eat those at lunch," Mia isn't going to stop trying to make the trade—she'll simply stop telling Mom. Instead, Mom can listen and provide lunch-trading strategies. Then, at another time, she can teach about best practices around eating candy. Life lessons go down much smoother when you slip them in at a later date—trust us, we do it all the time.

Interrupting vs. Echoing

Mastering the skill of echoing takes time and practice, but the rewards are worth it. Fortunately, kids give you a hundred opportunities a day to work your way to pro level. Let's look at the impact of echoing on the following conversation. Observe the difference between when this parent uses the tool and when they don't.

We asked a parent, "What do you normally do when your 9-year-old gets in the car and says someone was mean to her that day?" She broke down the conversation for us, warning us that she's still something of an echoing novice:

Mom: "How was your day?"

Jia: "Vihaan was mean to me today!"

Mom: "What happened?"

Jia: "She called me a stupid name in front of other kids, and everyone laughed."

Mom: "What was going on when this happened?"

Jia: "Well, I mean, umm, well, we were all in the hallway between classes."

Mom: "Well, did you tell her to stop?"

Jia: "I mean, no—there wasn't really a chance."

Mom: "What do you mean there wasn't a chance? What happened after? Why didn't you walk away?"

Jia, now looking down at her lap: "I don't know."

Let's see what might have happened had she tried echoing:

Mom: "How was your day?"

Jia: "Bad. Vihaan was mean to me today!"

Mom: "Ugh, Vihaan was mean today."

Jia: "She called me a stupid name in front of other kids, and everyone laughed."

Mom: "Aw, other kids got involved. That sounds embarrassing."

Jia: "Yeah. I wanted to run out the door and straight home."

Mom: "Man, you were so mad you could have run all the way home."

Jia: "We were in the hallway between classes, so no adults heard."

Mom: "You didn't get help, huh?"

Jia: "No."

Mom: "Man, that's rough. Do you want to talk more, or would you like ideas for what to do next time this happens?"

Echoing with More Than One Child

This one will sound familiar if you have two or more kids. One child says, "He did it. Not me! Why am I always the one who gets in trouble? You never get mad at him!"

Let's take a moment of silence for sibling rivalry. You might say, "You feel like you always get in trouble and not him."

As natural as it is, this kind of competition can wear you out. You don't need to fix their feelings or make them disappear. Even in these moments, each child will know they are being heard when you simply echo what you hear.

Take the example of Noah, age 8, and Gabe, age 6, who are close, but the big competition in their house is about who is best at whatever they're doing. When they start to argue, Dad steps in, echoing and using our coin toss recommendation:

Noah: "He cheated at the game; Dad, I saw it!"

Gabe: "He always says I'm cheating when he's losing."

Noah: "That's because you cheat!"

Gabe: "I do not! Dad!"

Noah: "Yes, you do!"

This conversation is going nowhere fast, and Dad knows regardless of what's happening, both boys are upset. So, he says, "Let's flip a coin for who gets to talk first. Only the person with the coin can talk for one minute, then the other person gets to hold the coin and give their side." This calmed the fighting down. Now, Dad took a deep breath and was ready to echo.

Gabe called heads and won:

Gabe: "I was playing, and he moved the piece to the next spot. I saw it, Dad. It was supposed to be four spots, but he pushed it to five. He was cheating, Dad!"

Dad: "I see you're frustrated because you feel like your brother cheated."

Gabe: "Yes, he did, and he should get in trouble if he cheats."

Dad: "You want fair punishment in this house for cheating."

Gabe: "Yeah. He should get in trouble."

Dad gave a knowing "mmm" sound and nodded: "Thank you for sharing your feelings. Time is up. Now, Noah, tell me what happened to you."

After a few more echoes back and forth, they did not solve the mystery of who, if anyone, had cheated, but both boys calmed down after their dad listened to both sides. What they needed was some breathing room and to be heard.

Be Open to Feedback: The Final Frontier

Your child needs to be able to tell you how you are doing as a parent even when it stings. Give them opportunities to tell you what you can do better. If they say, "You never listen," echo that!—"I haven't listened to what you're trying to say." Be receptive to their criticism and feelings about you and trust that there's truth to it from which you can learn and grow. This is perhaps one of the most complex challenges in the entire book. The "final frontier," so to speak. Be open to receiving feedback. Ask them, "What kind of listener am I?" or "What do you need from me when I upset you?" When you're ready to listen without getting defensive, ask them, "What can I do better as a parent?"

Ask them about your parenting and echo what they say even when it's incredibly hard to hear or you don't agree. Parents who are open to feedback from their kids grow an incredible bond. Take a deep breath and know that even if they have harsh things to say, having honesty between you will ultimately make you closer and put them at ease.

The Exception: When a Conversation Returns on Repeat

Sometimes, a child will return to the same worry and ask you for a solution again and again. You may feel like you've reassured them enough times, or you've talked through hundreds of strategies for thinking about it differently, and they're still stuck. Although it may seem like reassuring a child about the same fears helps them feel better, you may find that you only relieve worry in the moment and the concern often comes right back.

If you notice this happening, help them use an emotional regulation tool to find calm instead of getting stuck in the same conversation loop with you. Tell them, "It sounds like a fear is caught in your brain. Instead of talking about the worry, let's pause and use a chill skill to see if we can bring the worry down that way."

Engage Like a Pro Skills Cheat Sheet

◆ **Find the right settings:** Prepare yourself and start up conversations in your child's favorite places.

◆ **Keep your cool:** Don't overreact; it shuts down conversations. Use your calming tools.

◆ **Validate:** Let them know that you really understand their feelings.

◆ **Ask what they need:** Find out whether it's a listening ear, a hug, or words of advice.

◆ **Say simple things to keep the flow going:** Say "mm-hmm" without judgment in the delivery.

◆ **Express interest:** Ask, "And then what happened?" or "Wow, can you tell me more?"

◆ **Wait for natural pauses:** Speak once your child has finished talking. Don't rush or interrupt; give them time to find solutions.

◆ **Echo:** Pick out salient points and reflect back only what you hear.

◆ **Give positive feedback:** Tell them how appreciative you are that they shared.

After the Fact

Just like it's important to communicate skillfully during a conversation, what you do afterward is meaningful, too. Build trust with your child to ensure more open conversations.

Don't Gossip

Elena came to the group one afternoon telling us how her daughter was furious when she learned that Elena had talked to another school parent about her daughter's friend drama. Privacy becomes a bigger deal to children as they approach middle school, and we know from our therapy sessions that youngsters with parents who divulge their personal information often become more reserved. It's important to honor your child's requests for confidentiality, especially when they explicitly ask for specific details to be kept between you and them. While you may have that one friend you depend on who keeps things to themselves, exercise caution. Telling others about your child's most personal concerns is a breach of trust and could hinder the open communication you're working to maintain.

Repair When Communication Goes South

Children feel unseen when someone misses what they've said or is unavailable for a conversation. If a child feels disregarded repeatedly, it creates distance between you and eventually erodes your relationship. If you feel guilty for overlooking them when they needed to talk, forgive yourself and tell your child, "I missed what you were trying to tell me yesterday, and I wanted to make time to talk about it." If you talked and the conversation got heated, refresh your repair skills from Chapter 4, and be sure to apologize for your behavior.

Give Positive Feedback

It's essential to affirm to your children about speaking up and sharing regularly, and that seeking your help and advice is a strength, not a weakness. Simply say, "Thanks for being brave and sharing your emotions. That's not easy to do."

Follow Up

Show that you value what your child has shared with you by asking them how their friend is feeling after being bullied in gym class for being trans. Even if video games aren't your thing, ask, "How's your strategy working out for balancing your quests?" They don't have to have answers; it's more about you showing them you are thinking about what they said. Tell them, "I thought about how you told me I get too mad when you don't do chores. I'm going to work on that! Is there anything else you want to tell me?"

· · ·

Kids need a space where they can talk openly without feeling judged. When you engage with your children using this approach, you help them navigate life's challenges. They'll see you as a supportive and understanding figure, which can reduce their stress and anxiety. Using the Engage Like a Pro method strengthens your bond with them. So, be ready to apply these techniques in your next conversation with your child—you'll find plenty of opportunities to connect more deeply.

Questions and Reflections
for Deeper Thinking

Communicating as a parent isn't easy, so here's some space to explore your patterns. Maybe some topics make you uncomfortable or anxious when they come up in conversation, or you notice habits you have that hinder effective communication. Consider what's working, what needs improvement, and how you might better encourage your children to freely express themselves.

• What topics do you find the most challenging to discuss casually or without becoming overly distressed? What's something your child brought up recently that you found hard to "play it cool" about?

• How did the ways in which adults spoke to you as a kid influence your current conversation style?

• Considering what you know about your children, what do they need from you to feel at ease in a conversation? How do you typically react when they don't want to talk?

• What's your biggest challenge in having difficult conversations with your child? How might you be unintentionally shutting them down or discouraging them from opening up?

Seven

Role Model

So far in SAFER Parenting, you've learned how to help your child move through worry by setting your tone and helping them find calm. You've learned how to accept their emotions while guiding unhelpful behaviors and how to support them in forming a strong identity and sense of self. We have also demonstrated the mechanics of engaging like a pro.

But one of the most impactful things you can do for your anxious child is also one of the hardest, and we've saved it for last: role modeling healthy coping skills.

Most parents in our groups have started new healthy habits: Christina dives into elaborate cooking recipes when she's worried; Tasha starts her day with a short gratitude list. Others get relief from indoor gardening, using aromatherapy, or going for a run.

Some parents discover that the ways they manage their emotions and behaviors are rooted in their childhoods. Savannah finds herself very strict and rigid from growing up in a military family and always being the new kid in school. She told the group, "I rely too much on wine to relax; my mom was exactly the same." Garrett, on the other hand, picked up a habit of dashing out in moments of tension because it was the only way he could get space from his abusive father when he was young—by locking himself in his room. When he and his wife argue, he bolts as soon as tensions get high.

Helpful or not, these ways of managing our feelings and subsequent behaviors get learned somewhere. You want your children to mimic your healthy coping habits, even when you're still in the process of healing and learning to manage life differently. In this chapter, we'll show you how to model healthy coping mechanisms and guide children amid ongoing struggles that need long-term support.

Your Child Will Do as You Do, Not as You Say

Here's the reality: kids will mimic almost everything you do, even when you tell them explicitly not to. There's no world where you can behave one way and expect them to act another. It just doesn't work that way, and how you behave in front of them tends to be much more impactful than what you say.

So, if you want to see your kids calm down in moments of anxiety and overwhelm, then you have to model emotional management yourself. If you wish for your 6-year-old not to scream, "I hate pancakes!" when he can just as easily say, "I'd really like cereal this morning," you must learn to take a deep breath when you feel your frustration rising. If you snap at your partner every time they ask you to take out the trash instead of expressing your feelings constructively, then your child learns that being short and mean is an acceptable way to communicate with their loved ones.

The way you live, the choices you make, and the level of attention you pay to your mental health and well-being matter for both you and your kids, because they absorb your habits. Having a parent who models good coping skills decreases a child's worry over their lifetime.

Rather than taking the role of a professor at a blackboard, we want you to demonstrate *to* your children the values and expectations that are important to you and that you wish to see reflected in them. As a parent, it's essential to lead by example, but don't think you have to be perfect; that's never the goal.

Every parent suffers and struggles. What you see on social media and in the news of moms and dads doing it "right" is staged and made up. So, as you read this chapter, forgive yourself and move forward if you have been role modeling unwanted behaviors or speaking in ways you shouldn't. Don't forget that we often model what was modeled to us by our parents. They, too, have inherited coping mechanisms and passed them along to you, whether they admit it or not.

Change takes time at any age. When parents begin to see how their unproductive behaviors affect their children, they often feel an overwhelming sense of shame and guilt. Alessia told us, "Friday night dinners with my parents are the worst. My middle child invariably has a meltdown in front of everyone. I feel everyone's eyes on us as I try to soothe him. What's worse is I know he's copying me when I get angry, because I've lost it on him a lot. It crushes me."

We know it's hard to see your child struggling with the same things you do. But it's not all bad news! You will also pass along wonderful traits. One day, you'll notice that they have an ability with a sport or the same dimples as you. They'll be kind or compassionate like you, organize their stuff similarly, and may have the same funny clap when they get good news. Just like you can pass on those beautiful parts of you, you'll also pass on what you still need to work out.

Model That	Get This
Say, "I had a really hard day today."	Kids who put big feelings into words
Rant when plans get changed	Kids who are resistant to new ideas
Show that you can do hard things	Kids who build resilience to bounce back
Answer your phone at the dinner table	Kids who are distracted when you speak to them
Take a deep breath in traffic	Kids who slow down when stressed
Apologize to your kids when you snap	Kids who make amends when they hurt others
Complain when your kid loses a match	Kids who are sore losers

Roadblocks to Role Modeling

Sometimes, we find less than favorable ways to manage our feelings when uncomfortable. But remember, all behaviors impact mental health. If you're flooded with stress, anger, or depression and come home on autopilot, your inner feelings will come out in unsafe, unskilled, and anxiety-provoking ways. Your kids don't know what may be troubling you, but they watch how you conduct yourself.

Let's look at the most common roadblocks to role modeling and learn what to watch out for.

Addiction

People often turn to substances to cope. They feel like they're just letting off steam or relaxing after a hard day, though when it becomes a regular occurrence, underneath it is a way of coping with complex emotions and trauma—when we numb ourselves, we feel our emotions less strongly. Maybe you saw it growing up, as Rema did. They told the group, "My dad always had a few scotch and sodas every night. Now, it's my way of escaping the day's difficulties. I feel my anxieties melt away when I drink."

Luca shared Rema's sentiment: "I'm afraid I'm going to screw up my kids because my job is so overwhelming, I smoke a joint every night just to be able to unwind enough to sleep. My kid is watching me do this, and I know I'm sending the wrong message. I don't want him to become an addict."

Kids who see their parents smoking, even when they're told it's a bad habit, may find their way to the same behavior early in life. And if you repeatedly say to your children, "Today was hard; I'm going online shopping," this thinking will become a truth of life for them: we escape into something else when we feel uncomfortable.

Avoidance

Shying away from something—whether that looks like avoiding friends or family, neglecting doctor's appointments, or putting off dealing with your mental health—makes what's already difficult to deal with much more complicated in the long run.

This may be surprising, but getting overly engrossed can also become a way to sidestep other issues. Diana says, "I get so absorbed in research and emails that I lose track of time and miss dinner and bedtime with the girls. Often Mahmud, my husband, is asleep, too, so we never connect." For another parent struggling, it looks like watching TV all night in the living room for days on end because of her worry. You might be super anxious and just want to relax, but if you let this become a habit, your kids will learn that they need to escape to feel better when they are hurting.

Social Media

If a parent places too much emphasis on social media for their own self-esteem or constantly worries about others' opinions, their children are likely to notice and may adopt similar attitudes. When you frequently compare yourself to others or post online and check your device for notifications in front of your children, they can easily inherit an over-fixation on what others think of them, consistently increasing anxiety.

Defeatist Statements

Kids notice when you speak negatively about yourself, berate yourself for minor mistakes, or say things like "I can't get anything right." During an afternoon in a large parenting group, one dad said, "You know, I am really hard on myself. When I think back, I can remember that my dad always put his work first, and unless he landed a big construction job, I could always tell he was down on himself. We'd hear him mumbling, "I'm such an idiot good-for-nothing," when he missed out on a job. I pushed myself hard and am proud of what I've achieved for myself and my family, but I just realized I've said the same thing to myself all these years—that I am nothing unless I succeed."

Kiera anguishes over her every parenting move or worries that an officemate doesn't think she works hard enough. She told the group, "I constantly ruminate about the choices I've made in the past and stress about the future. I repeatedly sit in front of my children, deflated, and go on and on, 'How did I make that stupid mistake on the spreadsheet?' or lamenting about office politics and how I handled my latest meetings."

If you find yourself stuck on something or have difficulty letting go, watch out for falling into powerlessness about life decisions in front of your kids. They'll take this resigned thought pattern and run with it in their mind, thinking similarly to 9-year-old Hina, who said, "If I had only let the kid sit next to me at lunch last month, we'd still be friends."

Body Image–Related Behaviors

Children listen to you when you are mean to yourself and your body. They hear you when you say, "I feel fat!" or "No clothes ever look good on me." As children hear what you say, your voice becomes their way of thinking about themselves. It becomes all they know. They don't have the same discernment abilities we do; they think, "If Mom feels that way, then it must be true about me, too." It becomes a script repeatedly playing in their head, and they gradually believe the message without even trying.

If you are somebody who restricts certain foods and says, "I don't eat this because it'll make me gain weight," it's likely your child will not learn to eat in ways that healthily fuel their bodies.

Children may find it hard to appreciate their bodies if parents don't speak favorably about their own. It's common to have a complicated relationship with your body. You might find it hard to talk positively about yourself because you don't care for your skin, facial features, or current size. We want to bring your awareness to how you speak since kids imitate their parents, and it can have a significant impact on their mental health.

Dieting is not recommended for children, as it can lead to eating disorders, is ineffective for long-term weight loss, and does not provide the essential nourishment for healthy growth and development. If you're the one who's dieting, children pick up on those habits very quickly. If they see you skipping meals, saying you need to lose weight, or making a show of not eating certain foods to save calories, it registers with kids. And if you over-exercise, be aware that they pick up on that, too. Everyone has their own relationship with food and weight, but we urge you to think about how your challenges show up for your children. Yumi told us, "I've stressed over my body weight my whole life; my mom did, too. I know my daughter must be picking up her fear of weight gain from me. It feels like a never-ending curse passed down through generations." We understand, and we also know you can break those patterns.

• • •

Don't beat yourself up if you've been role modeling unwanted behaviors or speaking in ways you wish you hadn't. If while reading a passage in this book, you've thought, "That sounds like me!" then you'd be just like all the other parents in our groups—

you're human, you're learning, you're striving to be a better mom, dad, grandparent, or caregiver.

Coping habits can be passed from generation to generation, and chances are your role models passed their share to you. But we know how much kids thrive in safe and supportive environments, so do your best. We all have unhealthy habits and emotional roadblocks. All you can do is commit to taking a fresh approach. We're here for you, supporting your efforts to consistently use your new SAFER Parenting tools.

Model Good Coping Habits

Children are keen observers—they learn to take care of their minds and bodies by watching the grown-ups. The best thing you can do as a parent is to model a balanced approach to good health—both mental and physical—while surrounding yourself with a supportive community. Parenting is your chance to lead by example on all these fronts.

Think back to what a certain family member may have done to find calmness in their lives. Isabel told us, "I realize I'm just like my godmother with her painting. She was from the coast, so you could always find her, and now me, painting away on some beach scene." Richard said that every Christmas when they visit his dad, he's always tinkering with his 1970s Volkswagen bus in the garage. Richard told his daughters, "You know, they didn't have meditations online back in Grandpa's day, but I'm pretty sure this helps him stay peaceful; it's like his own little calm routine," and winked.

We've talked a lot about behavior and habits to keep in check as parents. Here are some coping strategies to embody in view of your children. These are meant not only to help you, but also to plant essential seeds in your child's psyche about how to handle stress for their lifetime.

Show and Tell

Find what coping skill works for you genuinely, do it in front of your kids, and talk to them about the benefits. For example, Angelica told her daughter, "I'm so annoyed by the neighbors stomping around upstairs. To help calm my nerves, I'm going to do that thing where you dunk your face in ice." Let your child watch you submerge your face into a bowl of freezing cold water and don't be afraid to laugh about it together as water drips from your eyebrows.

Everybody has helpful methods of managing their emotions. We want you to notice yours and lean into them. Tell your child what your practices do for you: "Knitting helps me relax after a hard day." Incorporate these occasionally into your regular conversations.

Physical Activity

When you exercise, you not only gain rejuvenation but also show your children that physical activity and connecting with nature are valued in your family. Share with them the benefits of movement and spending time outdoors. Amit's mom likes to play pickup basketball in the park when she can. She told her kids, "It clears my head to get a good sweat on."

Make plans to take a salsa class with your friend and tell your child how great it is to socialize while keeping your body moving: "When Danielle and I go out dancing together, we get to exercise and have fun at the same time!"

On the flip side, watch out for fixation on exercise: if you are freaking out that you didn't get to go to the gym one day this week, it models inflexibility to children.

Show You're Not Afraid of Your Own Worry

When your feelings are overwhelming, show your children that you can tolerate them. Let them see that emotions, even big ones, are manageable. Say things like "My heart is racing, which makes me feel jumpy, but I know what to do to help!" Help them see that feelings come and go, and it may take a few minutes or a day to feel better. As kids grow, they'll think, "I'm not afraid of feeling uneasy. Mom says she gets mixed up inside, but it always passes."

Tell Your Child Your Plan

If you feel your emotions escalating and your child needs you, communicate calmly about your anxiety and how you're handling it. In a nonthreatening tone, tell them you need to take a few breaths and that you'll be back in a minute. Say, "I feel my stress rising; I'm going to take a break and get my brain back into problem-solving mode. I'll meet you in the living room." Or say, "I know I sound frustrated right now, but I'm not angry at you. I'm concerned about something that happened at work." Then, go to your bedroom and take a thirty-second break.

Speak as You Want Them to Think

It's essential to be aware of your own speaking and thinking patterns, as children tend to follow suit. Like everything else, the first step is to bring awareness to these thoughts. With understanding, there can be change.

What children hear will become the cassette tape (excuse us while we age ourselves) that plays in their minds. Kids are constantly picking up on what you say and trying it on for size. Let the inner voice they develop from hearing yours be a positive one. You have a lot of influence on how your child feels about themselves.

Speak Positively About Your Personality

Let's talk about modeling your own positive identity. As we explained this to a group, Lien said, "This sounds challenging. My parents were so modest." We're not talking about bragging per se, but rather recognizing your positive traits so your children can learn to do the same. Let them see and hear you admiring yourself and your positive qualities, like "I am creative—I sculpt and make beautiful things from clay," or "I'm a good friend because I always listen carefully and remember details about people's lives." Don't back down from acknowledging your achievements. Compliment your efforts: "I'm proud of myself for figuring that out. That was a tough one!"

If you feel the impulse to complain about yourself or others, pause! In those moments, pivot by acknowledging your strengths instead.

Speak Positively About Your Body

Paige never wanted to have her picture taken, especially not after the birth of her second child. When her daughter refused to be in photos at her most recent birthday party, she came to us for advice. "I never realized she was picking up messages about herself when I talked about dissatisfaction with *my* body," she told us.

When it comes to your body and appearance, speak positively and say things like "I love my strong arms, they helped me carry you all those years." Wear a bathing suit, and don't scrutinize yourself in front of your children. If you catch yourself about to criticize your shape or weight, pause and think, "I'm about to put myself down in front of my child." Then make a different choice. Replace negative thoughts with loving and affirming language.

When it's hard to speak positively about what you look like, focus on the great things your body can do: "My body really helped me get through the day today. Riding my bike up that hill was tough, but wow, our bodies are amazing machines, aren't they?!"

Model Self-Empathy

Recognize out loud that everyone has imperfections. Instead of saying, "I'm so awful at baking; I always burn the bottoms," try something more compassionate, like "Even though other moms can do things like baking effortlessly, I teach you guys about the outdoors. That's where I shine, and I don't have to be the best at everything." And guess what—you can rewire your brain that way. It really works!

Be Positive and Hopeful

Acknowledge what's going well, even in challenging situations, like "That was tough, but I got through it." Speak with optimism, suggesting that positive outcomes are expected. Say out loud, "Of course I'll get what I need done, it just might take a bit longer than I expected." When negative thoughts arise, remind yourself, "I've had this thought before; I don't need to linger on it," and shift to a more neutral or optimistic perspective. With consistent practice, such pessimistic thoughts will become less frequent.

Model Courage

Kids with future-based worries need to see you tackle challenges: "I have a big meeting tomorrow, and being in front of people always makes me nervous, but I know I can take some deep breaths and do it." Kids have a harder time trying new things if they're worried about failing, so be vocal about your defeat, too: "I didn't make the qualifying time cutoff for the marathon this year, and that's OK!"

Navigating Deeper Challenges

Perpetual challenges are a shared part of the human experience, and no parent is excluded from this. But the sad truth is a child's anxiety often mirrors the unresolved turmoil in the family unit. It's as though children become conduits, the pathway transmitting the feelings of unease they sense from their parents. The powerful flip side to this is that as parents engage in deep, introspective work to address their own struggles, we see a remarkable transformation in children. In other words, when a parent heals, a child's anxiety often begins to dissipate.

We know you are committed to helping your child and probably already realize that some aspects of your well-being need ongoing attention. Use the following skills to talk about mental health, physical concerns, and changes in your family and to address the parts of you that are still a work in progress.

Seek Support for What You Can't Manage Alone

Suppose you or someone in your family is dealing with a long-term issue, such as depression, constant family disputes, or addiction. The first step is to devise a strategy to support the adults involved.

For instance, Courtney, a mom in the lunchtime parenting group, was struggling to curb her online gambling habit. She told us, "I come from a line of gamblers and I'm scared my kids are going to inherit this problem." The parents in this group had been working together for two months; they had formed a bond but were still getting to know one another. We asked Courtney if she'd be willing to hear suggestions from the others on supporting her healing, and she agreed. A few urged her to start seeing a therapist, and someone recommended free groups for addiction. Lucia invited her to join an online yoga class she takes on Wednesdays. Maurice said, "You always talk about how overwhelmed you are. Do you do any of the calming skills we've learned?" She said, "Honestly, not consistently." So they helped her set small actionable goals, like reaching out to a friend each day or going for a walk around the block.

Courtney was teary at the end and said, "Thanks, everyone; I feel like this is manageable, even though I know I'm a ways away from overcoming the urge to check my teams and bets online every day." At the end of the session, she agreed to take these small steps, and we thought it was a great place to start. Plans for healing should be attainable, and you should work toward your recovery by actively taking care of yourself.

Work through grief, trauma, and your own challenging emotions out of your children's sight, and do that work for yourself and your family. You may have had a cruel childhood or find yourself unable to manage your emotional reactivity, or your marriage is on the rocks. The effects of difficult times in our lives don't just vanish; they require patience and understanding. Whatever the situation, you deserve to heal. Don't try to ignore the problem. Otherwise, showing up for your children will become more difficult, if not impossible.

If you need support, be a SAFER Parent and model getting it. You can ask for a recommendation from a friend or trusted colleague, check out an online directory, or talk to your doctor about individual, couples, or group therapy. When you seek professional help, it normalizes going to therapy for your child, too.

If you have a physical condition, you should go to a medical professional and outline a course of action. Otherwise, it can become an undue burden on your children. Once in a while, share the broad strokes of your plan with your child. Melanie came to the group eager to tell us, "I called my doctor, and we're trying a new medicine regimen for my Crohn's; I thought it would cause my daughter anxiety to tell her, but she just gave me a hug and skipped away. It's the first time she seemed relaxed about it since my diagnosis two years ago."

Yasemin encouraged her husband to get outside help for his depression. He started weightlifting and saw a therapist twice a month. Reza had a partner who'd quickly go into a rage, and he learned to step away to take a break when his partner was too angry. Protect your child if a family member feels unsafe and make a plan.

Sometimes, you may have an adult at home who does not cooperate. If you live with a person who is volatile, seek guidance from a professional about the next steps to keep your child out of harm's way.

Tell Your Child What's Going On

As we learned earlier, children worry when things feel uncomfortable at home. They may be unable to describe exactly what's happening, but they can feel when something is off.

When we first meet parents for coaching, we often find out that significant things are happening in the family that they've never spoken about to their kids. But they're already aware, like Liam, age 8, who said, "I know Mom has anxiety. It's obvious." Nadia, age 12, said, "My parents aren't saying it, but I know they're going to break up. I hear them fighting every night. I've known it, like, forever." Some parents will read this book and realize they've never told their kids why a parent isn't in the picture, and you might have avoided the conversation up to this point.

Lily, age 9, told us, "Everybody acts like Grandma never has too much to drink, but she always does. I don't like how she talks to my mom, but all Mom does when I mention it is snap at me, 'Ignore it!'" Tearing up, she asked, "How can I ignore it when I know it makes Mom cry after Grandma leaves?" Many children with a parent who gets angry say, "We don't talk about it. We just pretend it didn't happen." When you keep the line of communication open, your children know they can depend on you to talk hard things through.

It bears repeating—they know. Kids see when your partner or family member upsets you, or when you act differently than usual.

Children need a way to make sense of more complicated things, and they need you to initiate these conversations. It might be hard to imagine how you could or why you would explain more adult subjects, especially when they are young. But age-appropriate transparency makes kids feel more at ease and helps them have less anxiety, no matter the subject. Review the skills on having difficult conversations in Chapter 3 before you share. If you have more than one child, you may need to have separate discussions for differently aged kids.

Perhaps you know you have a mental health diagnosis, or work stress is making you especially irritable at home, or you're like Latoya, whose grief became insurmountable after her father died: "I'd always heard that losing a parent leaves a hole in your heart that no one else can fill, but I never realized how true it was until now." Parents tend to wipe their tears away and say, "I'm fine, honey; I'm great," but their children can sense that something is off. You have good intentions—of course you don't want your child to worry. If someone is experiencing addiction and has slurred speech or personality changes when they use a substance, children will feel that, too. Parents often hope that if they don't draw too much attention to an issue, their child will be freed from the anxiety and stress of it. But the opposite could be true: your child could be worrying about it on their own because, as we've learned throughout this book, difficult situations are hard to hide.

Parents often ask why they must tell their children about something personal or complex. Kids need help understanding the particulars of adult concepts or issues because without talking to you they will fill in the blanks themselves and think, "My parents are ignoring this because it's too scary, too impossible; it makes them so worried that they can't even talk about it." Knowing you are there, calm and available to talk, turns you into the person who's safe for them to lean on and makes the unmanageable somehow manageable to them.

Some parents hope that if they keep the dialogue away, their children will be less likely to follow in their footsteps. Sometimes, it's quite the opposite—they will probably move toward those behaviors unknowingly. Remember, some information may be hard for your children to hear. They may have emotions, and that's OK; now you know how to Set the Tone, Allow Feelings to Guide Behaviors, and Engage Like a Pro.

Tell Them It's Not Their Fault

You can say, "Mom gets angry too quickly; she's working on it, but it's hard for her to stay calm sometimes—that's about her needing to work more on her emotional regulation skills, not about you." You might help your child understand a specific behavior in your extended family by saying, "Grandpa has extra stuff in the garage because it makes him feel safer; he always feels like he doesn't have enough because of how he grew up. We don't have to do that in our house. We are just fine without the extra supplies."

Context about what's going on helps lift the worry your child might feel about having caused it because children often think things are their fault. They can assume that arguments at home, and even divorce, are their responsibility. When kids talk to us in therapy, it sounds like this: "If I was ready for dinner when they called me down, they wouldn't have gotten into that big fight." Or Grayson, whose parents were getting divorced, told us, "If I had done my homework when Mom asked, she wouldn't have started sleeping on the couch."

Release your child from feeling responsible for things they have no control over. After working with us for a while, a parent with a complicated relationship with her brother shared with her 10-year-old son, "You might notice I act differently around Uncle Kieran; I am a little less playful. That's not your fault and has nothing to do with you. It's old stuff between us." Before she talked to him, she asked us, "He's so impressionable; will he think I don't love his uncle and cousins?" To her great relief, her son replied: "I could tell all along something was up! I love Uncle Kieran, but I don't like it when he bosses you around." Telling children age-appropriate facts lowers worry and anxiety, especially when they know they have you to talk to.

Morgan's older daughter had just returned from an inpatient treatment center for depression, so she explained to her 7-year-old, "Honey, your big sister's having a tough time and feeling pretty sad right now, but lots of therapists are helping her. I know it's so hard when she closes her door to you, and you wish she'd hug you as soon as she gets home. It's not because she doesn't love you; she's just dealing with her own feelings of sadness. If you ever feel uneasy or scared, you can come talk to me—I'm here to listen."

If you have a fight with your spouse in front of your child, you want to explain later that you recognize that fighting is not the way to go and know it must be unsettling for them. Tell them it's not about them. "Sometimes, Daddy and I fight, but we'll try to speak to each other more respectfully. It's never your fault." Otherwise, nine times out of ten, they will think it is.

If you notice your child likes to play referee or be a peacemaker at home, you can relieve them of the burden by saying, "It's not your duty to help us with our fight. We're responsible for finding ways not to raise our voices at each other."

When stressed, overtired, or generally at the end of your parenting rope, explain they are not to blame for your mood. On an off day, say, "I want you to know that if I ever seem upset or stressed, it's not because of you. Lots of things can make adults feel tired or grumpy." Meena shared with her son that she's had anxiety since she was a kid, long before he was born. He said back, "So, I didn't cause it?" Help them see that many things have nothing to do with them, even when they feel like they do.

As we've learned, kids take on blame for grown-up things all the time. Elizabeth, age 8, told us she could share the tools she was learning in therapy to "fix" her parents' marriage. One parent told us he remembers when he was 5, he thought he could help his dad not be so sad by doing comedy performances in the living room. It never helped his dad's depression, even though he tried for most of his formative years.

Focus on What's Being Done

Helping kids see that adult issues are manageable and that they're not their responsibility helps to lower anxiety and lets kids be kids. They like to focus on what's going right, so explain to them what's being done to improve the situation.

If you talk about mental health, you might say, "Dad's seeing a therapist to work on his anger and sleep issues. Just like we visit the dentist for our teeth, we talk to therapists for our mental health. In our family, taking care of both our minds and bodies is important, so Dad's getting help to feel better."

Explain to your children that you get outside support. Tell them, "Oh, I'm excited to talk through my stress about my new boss in therapy; I really like having someone who listens and helps me sort things out." Or take Erica, who told the group, "It never occurred to us to share with the kids that we meet with you. It's so helpful. Why wouldn't I want my kids to get counseling when they need it?" The following week, their preteen sarcastically quipped, "Duh, we hear you talk about Ashley and Maria all the time!"

Even if you are facing a tough challenge like eviction and you don't know where your next home will be, you can still tell your children what's in progress: "We're going to be moving, and your aunt is helping me find a place for us to live."

Often, spotting anything positive in a tragic situation can be difficult. Nevertheless, reassuring your children that they are not responsible for resolving the problem is essential, even if you are still figuring out how to handle it yourself.

Maybe you are working on obsessive-compulsive tendencies. You can take ownership by saying, "You might notice I'm always reorganizing the shoes or cleaning the counter when it's already clean. That's part of something I'm working on in therapy called OCD. It tells my brain to do things in a really specific way. It doesn't mean you need to organize your shoes in the same way I do, but I want you to know why I seem so focused on it."

If you are currently dealing with something you don't want them to emulate, teach and explain that there are better ways to cope. For instance, if you still smoke but want your child to understand the dangers of tobacco, inform them of the risks and explain that you're actively trying to quit while struggling with addiction. Move toward recovery, even if it's slow, and help your child make informed decisions later when offered a vape or cigarette.

Give Them Strategies to Manage

Make a plan for your kids and discuss what they can do when they are impacted by stressful situations at home or with other people in their lives. Refresh your memory of the coping tools in Chapter 4 before having this conversation.

Help your child develop strategies to self-soothe or step away when things get scary. Let your child know what to do when there is anger or conflict at home. "When your brother is angry, you can go straight to your room, shut the door, and use your calming tools. I will check on you and give you a special hug." Be sure to talk through a plan with your whole family so that everyone is on board.

Tell your child that from here on out, they can share with you how they feel—even if it pertains to you.

Say, for example, "If you ever worry that I seem sad, you can always come and tell me." If speaking directly is too intimidating for them, offer other ways to communicate: "If I ever upset you, or something feels too scary to say, you can write me a note rather than tell me in person."

If your child is having big feelings about what's going on at home, that's perfectly understandable. They may need extra help from a therapist or a support group designed to help children who are going through the same thing.

Help them find friends who can relate to their experiences so they feel less alone. Sam's dad died in combat when she was 6, and she went to a camp for kids who had lost a parent or close family member. On the car ride home, she said, "Mom, I met a girl who also lost her daddy." It was so helpful to be in a place with kids who understood how she felt.

In challenging circumstances, look into local programs and ask your doctor for resources. Tell your child there's no embarrassment in seeking support and that you would be proud if they took that step.

•   •   •

The importance of role modeling healthy coping skills for your children cannot be overstated. Yet, being a consistent mentor can be challenging when life is demanding. Prioritize your own mental and physical health to reduce your child's worry. Endeavor to consistently demonstrate the qualities and behaviors you wish to see in your children and be the family that talks about what's hard.

Questions and Reflections for Deeper Thinking

You did it! You've got the tools now to parent with more understanding, kindness, and self-awareness. Before we wrap up, take a moment to think about what you are role modeling. You're on your way to being a model of calm for your child, even when things get tough. So, as we close this chapter together, jot down your thoughts on raising calm kids in a world of worry—and let's keep this conversation going.

• What coping habits did you observe in your family members while growing up? Were any of these habits helpful, and others not so much? Do you model any of them as a parent today?

• How do you manage your stress and anxiety? How might your child's behavior be influenced by the way you cope?

• In what ways do you struggle to talk positively about yourself or your body?

• Have you considered getting help from a therapist or counselor to work through your emotions and develop healthier coping strategies? How would you describe any past experiences with mental health counseling?

• How can you help your child understand the worries or challenges in the lives of the people close to them? What age-appropriate explanations can you offer?

> • What new coping strategies are you planning to model?
>   How can you explain these efforts to your child to share
>   your commitment to personal growth as a parent?

• • •

Let's look at how one family implements all five SAFER Parenting skills.

Conclusion

Putting It All Together

Keanu and Leilani had come to realize that their relationship was no longer working despite their best efforts to maintain it. As a result, they decided to divorce. Their son, Liko, was 8 years old at the time, and despite their marital challenges, they were dedicated to using SAFER principles to help him manage this difficult transition. After becoming SAFER Parents like you, they had tools at the ready when it came time to address what had caused so much upset in the family for so long.

Understandably, both parents were nervous about the conversation. Mom was afraid she'd break down in tears, and Dad wanted to avoid the discussion altogether—he was angry with Mom for initiating the divorce and distressed that Liko would soon be bouncing between two homes. The couple focused on mastering Set the Tone as their foundational skill. With their communication now more strained than ever, it was vital to remain composed and reassure their son that, despite the significant changes ahead, they would get through this together.

Mom worked hard to control her emotions, while Dad recognized he needed to keep resentment and other feelings from overshadowing the conversation. They reviewed their SAFER

Parenting roadblocks, ensuring they didn't dismiss their son's feelings, lose their tempers, or try to minimize the situation.

First, Mom and Dad figured out what they would say and who would say what. Even this wasn't easy. Getting on the same page about anything felt challenging, but they found a way to align. They understood, from talking to us, the importance of maintaining consistency in the narrative they shared with their son. They wanted to make him feel secure by presenting a united front.

Mom and Dad chose to talk to Liko in the living room in the afternoon daylight and planned to do something less stressful together afterward—going to a park and then having ice cream at home. To calm their nerves before the conversation, each parent took thirty minutes to themselves while the other stayed with Liko. Dad went for a run, and Mom turned on soothing classical music and journaled.

We recommended they keep their language simple because Liko was only in third grade. When they all settled on the couch, with one parent on each side of their son, Dad placed his hand on Liko's knee and said, "We have some news to share—your mom and I have decided to get a divorce and live in separate places. Getting divorced means we won't all live in the same house anymore, but we will always be a family." Dad paused a minute to let the words sink in and to see if there was any immediate reaction. Liko didn't say anything, but he appeared interested, so Dad continued, "Sometimes, parents grow apart, but know that our decision has nothing in any way to do with our love for you or anything you did; it's between us grown-ups."

Mom glanced at her thumb and picked at a hangnail, while

Dad said more: "We are still your family, and our love for you hasn't changed. We'll each continue to make your meals, help you with homework, and tuck you in at night. We both have a special relationship with you. None of this affects how much you can love us or how much we love you, and you'll never have to choose between us. We'll always be your mom and dad."

By this point, Liko looked slightly shell-shocked. Neither parent said anything for a few seconds. Then Mom began to reassure him. She used her validation skills by saying, "It's OK if you feel sad or scared, and I know you might feel that way. Kids often feel sad, afraid, or even angry when their parents get divorced. Do you want to share what you're feeling?" They knew he'd likely express his real sentiments, especially since they'd been practicing SAFER skills with him for a year. He might even say something difficult for them to hear.

True to his bright personality, he said, "Actually, I hate it when you fight! Mom, you are so mean to Dad, and I don't like it." Mom felt horrible and wanted to blurt out, "Don't be mad; you'll now get to have two bedrooms with toys." But she knew that jumping to solutions would dismiss his big emotions. Instead, she reminded herself, "All I need to do is echo. Let me say back to Liko what I heard."

She echoed his feelings beautifully: "Buddy, I know you don't want us to live separately, and I also know it's been so tough at home. I should never yell at Dad like that. I imagine that must have been very scary for you."

Liko tried choking back his emotions, but he couldn't stop the tears as he sniffled out, "I don't want us to not live together!" He crossed his arms and dove almost completely into Mom's lap.

He hadn't done that in years. She held him close as she thought about how she might help him—at some point in the future—process his hurt feelings and sadness.

The three of them squeezed each other tightly for a few minutes. Then, Liko grabbed a blanket, snuggled up next to his dad, and looked up sweetly at his mom. Dad felt the urge to fix everyone's upset feelings, but he took a breath, listened, and made space for his son's words. He put his arm around Liko and said, "Budsters, I'm so sad about this, too, and we can talk about it as much as you want—today, tonight, tomorrow, or any day. We want to hear your thoughts, questions, and feelings about this. We are truly in it together."

After Liko's tears subsided, Mom and Dad went through some basic logistics to help their son feel prepared, letting him know that Grandma would still pick him up on Tuesdays and Thursdays, just like always. They also told him what day Dad would be moving into a new apartment. "One nice thing, buddy, is that Daddy's new place has a pool," Mom said.

Liko's parents had planned their routine with us ahead of time to provide consistency (we rehearsed it and collaborated with them on a script), so they could be clear about exactly which days he would be where. They showed him the new paper calendar of visitation days they had made. Later in the week, they began to familiarize Liko with Dad's new place by showing him the lobby of the building and talking about things like which paint color he might want to pick for his bedroom.

Although Liko was upset after the big talk, when they set off for the park, Dad and Mom felt they had done well. By the time they got home for ice cream, they all felt exhausted, and Dad later told us, "I'm mostly relieved to have it all out in the air."

When Mom got ready to tuck Liko in that night, she knew the topic of divorce would likely surface again because he tended to talk about his feelings before bed. That was his favorite time to share. She took some breaths to ground herself and walked into the room.

As Mom and Liko snuggled, he welled up again and said, "Mommy, what if I never stop crying before school on Monday?" She looked at him and echoed, "I know sometimes when the tears come, it feels like they'll never stop." He replied, "Yeah, like they'll never stop." She grabbed the teddy bear he'd had his whole life and talked like Paws: "Keep me tight tonight, and I will hold all your sadness." They both smiled and snuggled until he fell asleep.

Walking Liko to the bus in the morning, Mom asked him if he knew anyone whose parents had gotten divorced (even though she knew he did), and he mentioned his friends Riley and Cooper. She could tell it was important for him to see that his family wasn't so different from others and that he was not alone. She reminded him of the big community he has and reassured him that Saturday night dinners at his grandparents' house would stay the same.

Liko's parents also purchased books on divorce to read with him. On one of their car rides, Dad made a point to mention one of Liko's strengths amid the transition, saying, "I'm really proud of you. You knew exactly the screws we needed to finish your loft bed the other day. Nothing holds you back from completing a project." The hint of pride on Liko's face let Dad know that his praise meant something. Dad added, "You can always tell me when you miss Mom on our days together or if you're feeling sad."

As the weeks and months went on, Mom and Dad kept talking about the changes to help Liko feel SAFER and less worried during this significant disruption in his life. Even with some inevitable setbacks, this family transitioned smoothly to living in two places, and Liko feels comfortable talking to both his parents whenever he feels sad, angry, or confused.

A Letter to Your Child

Now that you've caught a glimpse into other parents' lives, we hope you come away knowing that every family struggles. You're not alone. Identifying problems, finding the right strategies, and role modeling behavior—this is an evolving lifelong project. Nothing and no one is perfect, so don't fret if your efforts on the path to SAFER Parenting are bumpy. Do your best, and always be willing to try again. The endgame is today. Be consistent, and just like Liko's mom and dad and the other parents and caregivers in this book, you'll get there!

Equipped with the knowledge and skills of a SAFER Parent, make this pledge to your children to help them navigate their worries with your protection. Share it with them.

> To my child,
>   I pledge to keep you safe in this enormous and sometimes scary world. I commit to being a calm place for you to return to when what is outside our front door intimidates or upsets you. I promise to be a place of compassion and unwavering support when worry overwhelms you. I will be your shelter, where you can feel protected and learn to believe in yourself.

I will show you that you can confide in me. When your troubles seem too much to bear, I will be there to share the weight. When tough things happen, we will talk about them. I'm here to listen with a tender heart and an open mind so you can express your thoughts and feelings without hesitation. No emotion or fear will be too small, and no topic will be off-limits. We will face all your worries together. I will help you understand and navigate difficult situations as calmly as I can. Even when things feel impossible, I won't forget that you are just a child trying to make sense of it all.

I commit to enjoying life with you and allowing you to shine in your uniqueness. No matter how different we may be, I will cherish every aspect of who you are. I will receive your individuality with openness and appreciation so you can experience unconditional love and grow proud of yourself. I will make our home a place where you can express yourself fully and authentically. I pledge to remain curious about things I don't understand and consistently encourage your interests. I will work to ensure you know I accept you exactly as you are.

I will envelop you with an extra layer of protection by weaving a supportive community of family, friends, and mentors into your life. They will be the fabric surrounding you and providing a safety net for you beyond our home. Our community will be a source of strength and inspiration, a reminder that you are never alone.

I acknowledge that I, too, am a work in progress, and I commit to working on myself just as I ask you to do. I will provide an example for you by using helpful tools to manage my own feelings. When I get mad, I will apologize.

I promise to infuse fun into our lives. I pledge to always find the time for us to laugh, play, and create beautiful memories together. I commit to helping you discover how wonderful life can be, from our most spectacular adventures to the smallest everyday joys.

I wish I could remove all the pain from your life, but I know it's impossible; so instead, I will stay with you until you feel better. I will not lie to you about the world to protect you, and I will be there to celebrate your every win and comfort you with every loss. I promise to listen closely to your worries and help you find ways to overcome them.

I vow to help you find courage to carry through life's adventures, and I know one thing for sure: you can always return to the strength of our bond.

Together, we can get through anything.

Acknowledgments

When we set out to do this project, we couldn't have imagined the effort it would take to complete it. Many wonderful people supported us along the way. Words can't do you justice, but here are a few:

Thank you to David Hochman, our beloved Edward Scissorhands, for shearing and trimming, even while on a travel assignment abroad. You guided us with your invaluable expertise from the book's inception to its final version, reliably chanting, "You are writers!" whenever we got insecure. This book would not have happened without you.

Anya Kozorez, your nurturing manner, poetic prowess, and editorial brilliance have earned you the title of our book's guardian angel. Your humor and calming presence during our eleventh-hour creative bursts kept us inspired and focused. Thank you for your unwavering support and loyalty, and for being our writing lifeline.

To Maria Shriver, whose profound commitment and monumental impact on the well-being of families and children have set a new standard for advocacy. Your belief in our message is the catalyst propelling our dreams forward. We set out to help as many families as possible, and thanks to you, parents worldwide will read this book and discover a greater sense of calm at home.

Thank you, Meg Leder, at The Open Field, for overseeing this project.

Deepest thanks to our extraordinary book agent, Shannon Marven at Dupree Miller and Associates, who has been our tireless advocate. Your steadfast belief in our work and exceptional business acumen have been instrumental in bringing this book to life. From the first phone call to the present day, your team's dedication, expertise, and passion have made all the difference.

Thank you to our editor, Nina Rodríguez-Marty, for leading us through the intricacies of Penguin Random House, step by step and email by email. We are incredibly grateful for your discerning vision and skillful organization of ideas. Special thanks to everyone at PRH who worked their magic behind the scenes to make this book a reality.

We want to extend our wholehearted appreciation to the following esteemed experts in their fields of psychology: Cori Rosenthal, LMFT (Eating Disorders), Rachel Gordon, LCSW (Child Development and Anxiety), Jacquelynn McLean Reid, LCSW (Diversity and Inclusion), Tamala Poljak, LMFT (Trans and Queer Parenting), Mark Troedson, PhD, LMFT, Jungian Analyst (Developmental Psychopathology), and Paul Silverman, LCSW (LGBTQ+ Identity). We sought your expertise for the superior knowledge and influence you bring to our field. Your profound insights have greatly enriched this book.

A big shout-out to our research assistants, Danny Choo-Kang at Barnard College and Victoria Frenner at Columbia University, who bravely ventured into the labyrinth of data and emerged with comprehensive ideas and research findings.

Endless and heartfelt gratitude to our family and friends, who tolerated hearing us say what feels like ten million times,

"We are working on the book." Thank you for your love and steadfast encouragement.

To each other: Many years ago, while sitting on a couch with cups of tea, we dreamed of combining our talents to help families thrive. Now we've achieved our ultimate goal—helping millions. Writing this book has been our most challenging endeavor yet, and we've done a lot. Here's to our dedication, sacrifice, and perseverance—we did it!

Index